Night Music

Poems

Dying: An Introduction (1968)

Scattered Returns (1969)

Pursuit of Honor (1971)

Hello, Darkness: Collected Poems (1978)

Essays

Innocent Bystander: The Scene from the Seventies (1975)

Night Music

POEMS

L. E. Sissman

Selected by PETER DAVISON

Foreword by EDWARD HIRSCH

A Mariner Original

HOUGHTON MIFFLIN COMPANY

BOSTON   NEW YORK   1999

First edition
February 1999

For information about permission to reproduce selections from
this book, write to Permissions, Houghton Mifflin Company,
215 Park Avenue South, New York, New York 10003.

Library of Congress Cataloging-in-Publication Data

Sissman, L. E., 1928–1976.
    Night music : poems / L. E. Sissman ; selected by Peter Davison ;
    foreword by Edward Hirsch.
        p. cm.
    ISBN 0-395-92570-3
    I. Davison, Peter. II. Title.
PS3569.I8N54 1999
811'.54—DC21   98-50890   CIP

The poems in this book were previously published in the following volumes:
Dying: An Introduction, Scattered Returns, Pursuit of Honor, and
Hello, Darkness: The Collected Poems of L. E. Sissman. Copyright © 1963,
1964, 1965, 1966, 1967, 1968, 1969, 1970, 1971 by L. E. Sissman.
Copyright © 1971, 1973, 1974, 1976, 1977, 1978 by Anne B. Sissman.

Acknowledgment is made to *DoubleTake,* where Edward Hirsch's foreword first appeared.

Book design by Anne Chalmers
Type: Perpetua, originally designed by Eric Gill
in 1929 for the English Monotype Corporation

Printed in the United States of America

QUM 10 9 8 7 6 5 4 3 2 1

Contents

from **Dying: An Introduction** (1968)

I.

II.

from **Scattered Returns** (1969)

I.

II.

from **Pursuit of Honor** (1971)

from **Hello, Darkness** (1978)

I.

II.

Brightness Undimmed:
L. E. Sissman (1928–1976)

"WE WERE NOT, either by temperament or experience, meant to live in paradise," L. E. Sissman wrote. It was for him a felt perception, a lived truth. Sissman's well-crafted, highly formal, densely packed verse has a quirky radiance, a wildly focused perspicacity, a verbal joyousness that sometimes evokes moments of perfect happiness, perfect health, but mostly inhabits a recognizably fallen world, a civic middle zone, a daily mid-twentieth-century American realm. He was a close urban observer, a cosmopolitan poet with a baroque sensibility and an omnivorous appetite for contemporary life, contemporary manners. He was part Randall Jarrell ("The Marschallin, Joy Street, July 3, 1949"), part Weldon Kees ("At the Bar, 1948"), part Frank O'Hara ("The Village: The Seasons"). Like Wallace Stevens, he was Orpheus in a business suit—a man who earned his living as an advertising executive by day, and his soul as a poetic maker by night.

Sissman had an ethnographic eye for his own era, his own realm. He was a sort of lyrical anthropologist of his chosen milieu, the Northeast Corridor. Reading his poems you can hear the commuters ordering Scotch and branch water in the terminal bar, you can see the landscape passing through the windows of the moving train. It is no wonder that John Updike has written so insightfully about him, both in prose and poetry, since he shares with Updike an ability to evoke a moment in time in all its shimmering particularity. Many of his poems have dates in their titles: "East Congress and McDougall Streets, Detroit, May 25," "December 27, 1966." They are moments lifted out of time, held aloft and immobilized in the permanence of print.

Sissman had a special gift for eliciting, somewhat ironically, his salad days in the 1940s ("Here I will entertain the young idea / Of Cambridge, wounded, winsome, and sardonic"). He faced the discouraging fifties, which were for him devoid of poetry, with a wry survivor's wit ("At last with you the first time in my life, / My anchor, my harbor, my second wife"). He wrote with sharp-eyed clarity and bright forthrightness about the mid-1960s and early 1970s, for him years of propulsive creativity in the face of a constantly approaching death ("Very few people know where they will die, / But I do: in a brick-faced hospital, / Divided, not unlike Caesarean Gaul, / Into three parts"). It was characteristic of Sissman to notice, in writing about his death place, that the hospital was split up like Julius Caesar's conquered territory, and to pun on the word "Gaul" (gall). He was quiet, urbane, and high-spirited. Behind it all, his poems shine with a restrained but very real human longing and passion. They have a ruthless authenticity. They live in time. They remember paradise.

Louis Edward Sissman was born in Detroit on New Year's Day, 1928. He was part Jewish, part gentile, a gifted only child with an enormous vocabulary and a prodigious appetite for facts. (His remote and peripatetic parents, both ardent socialists — a proud, good-looking mother and a hardworking but feckless father — stand on two sides of his selected poems like ushers at the mortal gates.) He would later recall with amusing clarity what it was like to be a quiz kid on the radio and, at thirteen, to compete in the National Spelling Bee in Washington where, as he put it, he "bested some poor little girl from . . . Kentucky on an easy word ('chrysanthemum,' as I remember) and became the National Champion, the emoluments of which office included a $500 Defense Bond, a wooden plaque with two bronze owls on it, and an all-expense-paid trip to New York." The passion for particulars is revelatory, like the disclosure that follows: "My main reaction to all this was to lose my lunch more frequently than usual, a long-standing symptom of my revulsion to performing in public, and to conceive a lifelong hatred for the exploitation of the young." Sissman's sense of his own vulnerability enlarged into a sympathy for the suffering of others. Irony was protective covering, and compassion runs like a secret current through his work.

Sissman entered Harvard in the fall of 1944. He once said that he had never felt the merest traces of belonging anywhere until he took the trip east to Boston. At sixteen he was tall and gangly (six foot four, two hundred pounds), awkward, footloose, romantic — a bohemian in the making. The former quiz kid had been soured by his experiences with teachers; he was intellectually precocious but emotionally unprepared for college. Bad grades and an insolent attitude got him booted out for a couple of years after the war. A dean reputedly said to him, "We have no room at Harvard for geniuses." (See "In and Out: Severance of Connections, 1946.")

Sissman got a job as a stack boy in the Boston Public Library, moved through a series of furnished rooms, pursued girls, wrote poetry, grew up. (See "In and Out: A Home Away from Home, 1947.") He was readmitted to Harvard in 1947, married for the first time in 1948, and sailed through to graduation *cum laude* in 1949. He won the Garrison Prize in poetry ("Canzone: Aubade") and was elected class poet. He matured under the tutelage of John Ciardi, Andrews Wanning, and Theodore Morrison; his primary poetic models were W. B. Yeats, T. S. Eliot, and, above all, W. H. Auden. His work is rife with allusions to all three. Like Auden, he was a civic poet with a taste for narrative and a gift for metrical forms, for unfolding poetic sequences. Perhaps his natural formality was a way of distancing and ritualizing experience, since he was always an explicitly personal writer.

The fifties were for Sissman an off-kilter decade as he struggled to find his way. He had what he called "a short, unhappy stint in New York." He worked as a copywriter and copyeditor at Prentice-Hall, got a different job, equally undesirable, equally underpaid, with a publishing firm that collapsed, and returned somewhat ignominiously to Boston, where he moved on the fringes of the demimonde and had a series of disconnected jobs (campaigning for John F. Kennedy, selling vacuum cleaners, etc.) until eventually he landed in an advertising firm, which he liked. Some of these experiences can be gleaned from his later poems, but he seems to have written no poetry for a decade. As his friend and editor Peter Davison has written, "Seen in hindsight his poetic silence is so curious as to be nearly as deafening as the seven-year silence that befell Wallace Stevens after *Harmonium*."

By the end of the 1950s Sissman had found his path. He started the decade as "Lou" and ended it as "Ed." He married for the second time, now happily, and he and his wife Anne settled in the far suburb of Still River, an hour west of Boston. He enjoyed the craft of advertising, where his verbal dexterity and quick wit, as well as his knowledge of products, of how things worked, stood him in good stead, and he worked successfully in it for the rest of his life. He was also intermittently writing poetry again, some of it revived from college notebooks. In "Writing, 1963" Sissman dramatizes with some precision the experience of awkwardly coming back, of being stirred into poetry again, into verbal life:

> Self-denying
> Can get you something if, behind the blank,
> Unwindowed wall, you don't become a blank,
> Unfurnished person. He was lucky. In
> The dark of those bare rooms to let, there stirred
> Something: a tattered arras woven with
> A silent motto, as Eliot said. A word
> Now, in his thirty-sixth summer, surfaces, leading
> A train of thought, a manifest freight, up to
> The metalled road of light—for the first time
> In ten disused, interior years—along
> The rusted, weed-flagged lines. And so the raid
> On the inarticulate, as Eliot said,
> Begins again.

The poet's pen had cut "its first / Orders in ages," heading off in an unknown direction, heading back to his past, out of step but picking up speed, and by 1964 he had assembled a typescript of poems entitled *Homage to Cambridge*.

In 1965 Sissman discovered that he had Hodgkin's disease, an incurable illness that he recognized as "routinely fatal," and thereafter worked with a palpable sense of time's urgency. Chemotherapy gave him intermissions of health for eleven more years. But he had been "introduced" to dying, and from then on wrote ardently, incessantly, as if his life depended on it. His days were numbered ("numbers" is an old name for poems) and he numbered them in return. This time the cocoon opened and the poet emerged. Or as he put it, "Instead of a curtain falling, a curtain rose. And stayed up, revealing a stage decked in defining light."

Sissman's first book was charmingly, touchingly entitled *Dying: An Introduction* (1968). It was as if his entire life had been a preparation for this honorable, somewhat formal meeting that would spur him into becoming the poet he was always meant to become even as it drained the world of its substance, of life itself. There is a breezy effortlessness to the epigrammatic

rhyming couplets and flexible blank verse lines weighed with earthly obser-
vations. "Death is the mother of beauty," as Stevens put it, and *Dying: An In-
troduction* has a verbal gaiety, a joyous exuberance, a sense of fleeting beauty
undaunted but deepened by fatal illness. It also has the gravity of late
knowledge, of memories saved from oblivion and held up triumphantly to
the light.

After his first bout with Hodgkin's, Sissman continued as the Creative
Vice President of Quinn and Johnson Advertising in Boston. ("Whatever I
gave at the office," he said about his sixteen years of fifty-five-hour work
weeks, "I received more in return.") He wrote a total of forty-five book re-
views for *The New Yorker* and fifty-five monthly columns for *The Atlantic
Monthly,* some of which he selected for a personable collection of essays, *In-
nocent Bystander* (1975). He published two more books of poems during his
lifetime, *Scattered Returns* (1969) and *Pursuit of Honor* (1971). He wrote
with an almost alarming fluency and technical skill until 1974, when his
health failed him again and poetry mysteriously deserted him. ("Poetry is
not like reasoning, a power to be determined according to the determina-
tion of the will," Shelley wrote. "A man cannot say, 'I will compose poetry.'
The greatest poet even cannot say it, for the mind in creation is as a fading
coal which some invisible influence, like an inconstant wind, awakens to
transitory brightness.") In the last years of his life Sissman sought and found
the humane psychoanalytic guidance and friendship of Robert Coles, but
poetry could not be wooed back. "The Muse has departed the body — look-
ing back on its quickening decline," he mused. It was true. He had reached
the summit.

Sissman had the foresight to provide a characteristically jaunty title for
his posthumously published collected poems, *Hello, Darkness* (1978), which
added thirty-nine poems to the oeuvre, including his final advancing self-
elegies, hospital dreams and late farewells ("Nowhere is all around us, pres-
sureless"). The book won the National Book Critics Circle Award and de-
serves to be remembered as one of the high water marks of American
poetry in the 1970s. He was forty-eight years old when he died in 1976.

I was eighteen when I stumbled upon *Dying: An Introduction* in a college
bookstore, and I still recall the frisson of pleasure I got from the sheer glee-
fulness of the language, the youthful gaiety of intellect, emotion recollected
in frivolity and playfulness, with ironic wit and shivering undertows of feel-

ing. I liked the way S. memorialized his wisecracking college buddies and relayed his (often thwarted) romantic episodes, and I felt as if he were delivering to me my own present through his recollected past. I liked his funny but genuine way of honoring his literary predecessors, his irreverent allusions to Sappho ("where I lie, not quite alone") and Shakespeare ("Look, those/are spectacles that were his eyes"), to Coleridge and Yeats simultaneously ("A pleasure dome of Klees and Watteaus"), to writers I was just beginning to discover, such as William Dunbar ("Lament for the Makers, Including Me: 1967"). One learns from Sissman's example that the whole of poetry is available to us for our own use, our own enchantment.

Sissman has always had admirers and advocates in his own generation (in addition to Updike and Davison, one thinks of Anthony Hecht, Richard Howard, and Howard Moss, who published him so handsomely in *The New Yorker*), but he also deserves to be remembered by another generation. He speaks to us. He offers an encouraging vitality, a poetic style that is flexible, formal, and contemporary, dense enough to deliver the facticity of the world, wide enough to encompass its large realities. He favored the poetic suite, the discontinuous sequence, which allowed him to bring together the intensity of the short poem with the amplitude of the long one. He could zoom in on precise moments, particular locales ("The West Forties: Morning, Noon, and Night"), he could provide an overview for a generation ("A War Requiem"), even as he accrued a personal story, suggesting an autobiography. He provides an example of wit schooled by feeling and deepened by experience, of intellect coming together with restrained but warm underlying emotion, of poetic freedom enabled by expertise.

I've always been moved by the courageous and sometimes anguished playfulness with which Sissman faces the dark moments of experience ("Hello, black skull. How privily you shine / In all my negatives"). He is fanciful and unflinching, he sees everything through an "invisible new veil of finity." He knows that perhaps the closest we can come to paradise, almost always an unknowing paradise, is perfect health; conversely, a crushing mortal illness has its aspects of Hell:

> If Hell abides on earth this must be it:
> This too-bright-lit-at-all-hours-of-the-day-
> And-night recovery room, where nurses flit
> In stroboscopic steps between the beds

All cheek by jowl that hold recoverers
Suspended in the grog of half-damped pain
And tubularities of light-blue light.

Sissman understood what it meant to befriend winter while eliciting the memory of spring. His last poems show us a decent ethical man, a good citizen and "innocent bystander" looking with relentless honesty and clairvoyance at the harsh realities of his own passing. They are filled with poignant, tender, unremitting observations. In his final poem, "Tras Os Montes," he memorializes first the death of his mother (1892–1973), then the death of his father (1895–1974), and finally invokes his own rapidly approaching death (197-). That last open hyphen is a cruel stroke. He imagines climbing a mountain at first with his friends ("In Company"), then with his wife ("A Deux"), and finally by himself ("Alone"). In the end, the poet's hand "Reverts to earth and its inveterate love / For the inanimate and its return." These noble lines were his farewell and return. What L. E. Sissman wrote about W. H. Auden seems equally true about himself: "Like his idol Mozart, he made music that was formally grave and joyous without forsaking the human impulse, the human aspiration, from which it sprang."

EDWARD HIRSCH

from

Dying:
An Introduction

I.

Parents in Winter

I. MOTHER AT THE PALACE, 1914

In ragtime, when my mother ran away
From flat Ontario with Art to play
A fair Ophelia on the two-a-day
Time of that time, she was just seventeen
And far behind her figure and her face
In bearing, aim, and point: one more good kid
To swell a progress or to farce a scene
With slim impersonations of a race
Of royal losers, which is what she did.

Until, until. Until, in Buffalo,
The Rep played out its string and let her go,
And she tried out before the morning show
By gaslight in the cold Academy
For right end in the chorus, which required
An elemental sense of rhythm, and
A dauntless liking for variety,
And a good pair of legs, which she had. Hired,
She danced split weeks across the level land.

In Dayton, at the little Lyceum,
She was first billed with Andy as a team—
Shannon & Anderson—a waking dream

Worth thirty dollars weekly. Soon, in Troy,
Her act was spotted by Gus McAdoo,
Who made her both a single and a star
At twenty; and, in the blood-tasting joy
Of early triumph, barely twenty-two,
She played the Palace just before the war.

The times forbid me to imagine all
The grandnesses of that high music hall
Upon her opening, when, at her call,
Packards and Pierces inlaid new-laid snow
With their non-skid tread, largely loitering
While their Van Bibber owners drank her in
Through two-power pearl Zeiss glasses, in a glow
Of carbon-arc limelight wherein she sang,
En Dutch girl, to those white fronts that were men,

"When I wore a tulip." Many a rose
Made its red way toward her ravished nose
With its eleven peers and one of those
White cards of invitation and entrée
To a man's world of idleness and grace,
Leather and liquor and less fluent night
Exchanges than one would expect, and day
After day embowered alone to face
Oneself returning singly from the night.

"You great big beautiful doll," she sang, but "No,"
She said to her appraisers, who would go
To any lengths for her after the show.
I wonder why she did. Perhaps she saw
No commonness in their inheritance
And her upstart career; perhaps she felt
The condescension in their bids, their law
Of put and call. Instead, she chose to dance
And sing on in the hand that chance had dealt.

I wonder, too: was it her Irish pride
That made her tell the man she would not ride,
And so turn down a rôle with Bonafide
Films, Limited, and so turn down a road
That was to lead to giving up the stage
And taking up the piano, to her glory,
And winning the Bach prize, and having sowed
Such seeds and oats, at last to marriage,
And so to me? But that's another story.

II. FATHER AT PACKARD'S, 1915

The brick plant like a school. The winter set
Of East Grand Boulevard. The violets
Of dawn relent to let us see the first
Shift of its students hurrying to class
Distinction in the undistinguished mass
Concealing offices and cubicles,
Great drawing rooms with draftsmen on their stools,
Foremen's rude cabins bringing outdoors in,
Craftsmen's workbenches littered with their trim
Brushes and colors, and, in Main, the lines
Of workers in their hundreds vanishing,
With our perspective, at the end of all
The crucial stations in their longsome hall.
Here comes my father. Look how thin he is.
See snowflakes flower on the blank plat of his
Forehead. Note his black hair. In hand,
He has already all the instruments
(Pre-war and German in their provenance)
To tap and die a life. Intolerant
To the last thousandth, they encompass all
Protracted elevations of his soul,
And in their narrow ink lines circumscribe
The isometric renderings of pride
Which will propel him through the glacial years
While he designs the sun and planet gears.

East Congress and McDougall Streets, Detroit, May 25

Now winter leaves off worrying our old slum,
And summer comes.
Already docks,
Daisies and dandelions, thistles and hollyhocks
Begin to camouflage the tin in vacant lots.
(Some vegetable god ordains these plots
Of plants to rule the earth.
Their green clothes mask the birth-
Marks of a blight.)
Look down the street: there is nobody in sight
As far as Mount Elliott Avenue (where
We kids in knickers took a double dare
To hop a Grand Trunk freight;
Where, every night,
Those marvellous whistles came from).
This dead kingdom,
Composed of empty shanties under the sun,
The arc lamp swinging overhead (the one
That hung there in 1930), the same sidewalks
Of dog-eared squares of slate marked with the chalks
Of the persisting children, the sad board
Fences which shored
Up private property falling into the alley,
This was Jerusalem, our vivid valley.

In our dead neighborhood
Now nothing more can come to any good.
Least of all the Victorian orphanage that still stands
Behind an ironic fence on its own grounds
Diagonally opposite.
The convict children have forsaken it:
In one mad prison break, foiling their guards,
They burst out from its wards—
Long as the Hall of Mirrors, high as a kite,

Carved like a cuckoo clock, capped with grey slate—
Leaving an archive of curses on its walls,
A dado of dirt at hand height in its halls,
And a declivity in each doorsill.
Now the street-Arabian artillery
Has lobbed a brick into each gallery
And opened every window from afar.
Each outer door, ajar,
Is a safe conduct to the rat,
The mouse, the alley cat.
Under its exaggerated eaves,
The orphanage endures. Here nothing leaves,
Nothing arrives except ailanthus trees.

My thirst for the past is easy to appease.

Henley, July 4: 1914–1964

Fifty years after Capt. Leverett Saltonstall's Harvard junior varsity became the first American eight to win the Grand Challenge Cup at Henley in England, Saltonstall . . . will lead his crew back to the scene of its triumph. Every man who pulled an oar in the victorious 1914 Harvard crew, as well as the coxswain, is not only alive but is preparing to return to Henley on July 1. They will take to a shell again on the picturesque Thames course during the forthcoming regatta.

— *The New York Times*

Fair stands the wind again
For nine brave Harvard men
Sung by both tongue and pen,
        Sailing for Henley
Fifty years after they
Won the great rowing fray
On Independence Day,
        Boyish and manly.

On Independence Day
Fifty light years away
They took the victor's bay
    From mighty Britain.
They were a City joke
Till they put up the stroke
And their strong foemen broke,
    As it is written.

Leverett Saltonstall
Is the first name of all
That noble roll we call,
    That band of brothers.
Curtis, Talcott, and Meyer,
Morgan and Lund set fire
To England's funeral pyre,
    They and three others.

That young and puissant crew
Quickened their beat and flew
Past all opponents, who
    Watched them in wonder.
Fifty years later, we
See them across the sea
Echo that memory
    Like summer thunder.

Fair stands the wind again;
Thames, bear them softly, then.
Far came these rowing men
    In every weather.
What though their stroke has slowed?
(How long they all have rowed!)
Oarsmen, accept our ode,
    Blades of a feather.

A College Room: Lowell R-34, 1945

A single bed. A single room. I sing
Of man alone on the skew surface of life.
No kith, no kin, no cat, no kid, no wife,
No Frigidaire, no furniture, no ring.

Yes, but the perfect state of weightlessness
Is a vacuum the natural mind abhors:
The strait bed straightway magnetizes whores;
The bare room, aching, itches to possess.

Thus I no sooner shut the tan tin door
Behind me than I am at once at home.
Will I, nill I, a budget pleasure dome
Will rear itself in Suite R-34.

A pleasure dome of Klees and Watteaus made,
Of chairs and couches from the Fair Exchange,
Of leavings from the previous rich and strange
Tenant, of fabrics guaranteed to fade.

Here I will entertain the young idea
Of Cambridge, wounded, winsome, and sardonic;
Here I will walk the uttermost euphonic
Marches of English, where no lines are clear.

Here I will take the interchangeable
Parts of ephemerid girls to fit my bed;
Here death will first enter my freshman head
On a visitor's passport, putting one tangible

Word in my mouth, a capsule for the day
When I will be evicted from my home
Suite home so full of life and damned to roam
Bodiless and without a thing to say.

An orphan home. But into this eclectic
Mass of disasters sails Mrs. Circassian,
Maid without parallel, queen beyond question
Of household gods, gas and electric.

She puts the room right with a basilisk
Look, pats it into shape like a pillow;
Under her hard hand, the Chinese willow
Learns how to live with an abstraction. Risk

All and win all is her maiden motto,
Which makes mere matter fall into its place,
Dress right and form platoons to save its face,
And suffers Pollock to lie down with Watteau.

The Museum of Comparative Zoology

Struck dumb by love among the walruses
And whales, the off-white polar bear with stuffing
Missing, the mastodons like muddy busses,
I sniff the mothproof air and lack for nothing.

A general grant enabled the erection,
Brick upon brick, of this amazing building.
Today, in spite of natural selection,
It still survives an orphan age of gilding.

Unvarnished floors tickle the nose with dust
Sweeter than any girls' gymnasium's;
Stove polish dulls the cast-iron catwalk's rust;
The soot outside would make rival museums

Blanch to the lintels. So would the collection.
A taxidermist has gone ape. The cases

Bulging with birds whose differences defy detection
Under the dirt are legion. Master races

Of beetles lie extinguished in glass tables:
Stag, deathwatch, ox, dung, diving, darkling, May.
Over the Kelmscott lettering of their labels,
Skeleton crews of sharks mark time all day.

Mark time: these groaning boards that staged a feast
Of love for art and science, since divorced,
Still scantily support the perishing least
Bittern and all his kin. Days, do your worst:

No more of you can come between me and
This place from which I issue and which I
Grow old along with, an unpromised land
Of all unpromising things that live and die.

This brick ark packed with variant animals —
All dead — by some progressive-party member
Steams on to nowhere, all the manuals
Of its calliope untouched, toward December.

Struck dumb by love among the walruses
And whales, the off-white polar bear with stuffing
Missing, the mastodons like muddy busses,
I sniff the mothproof air and lack for nothing.

Stillman Infirmary

Clowning with you, I fell into Lake Waban
In late November and ended up in Stillman.
Was a loose kiss in the dark Agora
Worth such an earache and so much penicillin?

Why, yes. Where else was my grandmother's house
Open for business? Where else was the "in"
Sheet signed by three white shifts of nursing mothers?
Where else was food so innocent and filling?
Where else could wards make only children brothers?
Where else, if you were young and weak and willing
And suitably infected, would they ease you
Of all impediments except your childhood,
One almost insupportable snatch of river
Twisting to westward, and the smell of woodwork?

Today some civil servant must deliver
Us from all this strong languor and abolish
Our ultimate retreat, which he has done.

Passing the site, driving along the river,
I see apartments sprung up from the ashes
Of my late childhood. Farther east, the skyline
Is made and broken by a topless tower
Of wet white concrete painted by Dong Kingman.
Its name is Hygiene. Its mauve curtains shelter
New men who need not ever go to Stillman.

Clowning with you, I fell into Lake Waban.
I wonder where you currently are matron.
I wonder if you ever think of clowning.
I wonder if I could have stayed in Stillman.

In and Out:
Severance of Connections, 1946

1. Civis

Walking the town as if I owned it all—
Each lilac leafing out in Brattle Street,

Each green vane in the hollow square guarding
The gargoyles on Memorial Hall, each inch
Of rubber tubing in the Mallinckrodt
Chemical Laboratory, each
Particle who would learn and gladly teach,
Each English bicycle chained to its rack,
Each green bag humping on its scholar's back,
Each tally for a Cambridge traffic death,
Each boyish girl who makes you catch your breath,
Each Argyle sock, each Bursar's bill, each ounce
Of shag, each brick, each doctorate — as if
I owned the entire spring-wound town, I walk
Up the north path to University Hall.

2. *Magister*

The Master's teeth squeak as he sprinkles me
(Too hot to handle) with a mist of spit
That dries quite coolly. "Edwards, I've got some
Rough news for you." In his glazed, padded, blue
Old double-breasted serge suit and his bat-
Wing bow tie (navy, with pink polka dots),
He lets me have it right between the eyes,
His aces on the table, man to boy.
"Look, if there's one thing I can't tolerate
It's smart guys that won't work. The deans are soft
On geniuses. Not me. What we need more
Of is Midwestern athletes who get C's."
He stands up to reveal that his brown vest
Is perfectly misbuttoned. "Now, don't think
That I'm the least bit sorry about you.
I'm sorry for your mother and your dad.
You let them down. Now, you get out of here
And do something worthwhile. Work with your hands.
Stick with it two years. Maybe they'll take you back.
Okay, fella? That's it. Now let's shake."
We shake. I shake in secret with the shame of it.

3. *Exilium*

The ghost goes south, avoiding well-worn ways
Frequented by his friends. Instead, he slips
Into loose shadows on the sunless side
Of the least-travelled street. But even there,
One with a bony finger points him out
And pierces him with questions. Zigzagging,
He hedges hastily back to his route,
Which leads on past his windows, tendrilly
Embraced already by the outriders
Of summer's ivy, past his pipes and books
And dirty shirts and mother's picture, past
The dining hall where his name is still good
For a square meal, no questions asked, and past
The common room which is too good for him.
Across the Drive his beast heaves into view:
A monster boathouse lolling on the bank
Of the high river, backside in the water.
Inside, he greets the landlord's black-haired daughter,
Miss Jacobs, with a nod, and goes upstairs
To put his chamois-seated crew pants on.
Then, past the ranks of Compromises, he
Walks out to the land's end of the long float,
Selects his Single, and stands out to sea.

In and Out:
A Home Away from Home, 1947

1. *One O'Clock*

With gin, *prosciutto,* and Drake's Devil Dogs
In a brown-paper bag, I climb the Hill
On Saturday, the thirty-first of May,
Struck by the sun approaching apogee,

Green comments issued by the Common trees,
Mauve decadence among magnolias,
The moving charcoal shadows on the brown
Stone of the moving brownstone where I live,
And a spring breath of Lux across the Charles.
My key mutters the password; I step in
To the dense essence of an entire past:
Rugs, chicken, toilets, Lysol, dust, cigars.
Through that invisible nerve gas (which leads
In time to total incapacity),
I climb the two flights to my little flat.

2. *Two-Thirty*

Done with the Devil Dogs, I take the brush
Out of the tooth glass and decant my first
Gin of the afternoon. In half an hour
She will be here. All is in readiness:
The bedspread taut, the ashtrays wiped, a glass
Swiped from the bathroom down the hall, a small
Plate of *prosciutto* canapés. Now Fu
Manchu reclines at ease in his hideaway,
While his nets, broadcast, sweep their victim in
To an innocuous address on Pinckney Street.
Now Lou the Loser uses all his ten
Thumbs to count up the minutes till she comes,
Or till (more likely, with his luck) she never shows.
The gin sets up a tickle in my toes.
I blow my nose. The room is hot. A fly
Does dead-stick landings on my neck. She's late.

3. *Three-Ten,* et seq.

The doorbell rings. I barrel down the stairs
To meet the coolest copy I have seen
Of Sally on the steps. Up in my room,
I fix her gin and secretly survey

This manifestation by which I have so
Astoundingly been visited: a girl.
She walks on her long legs, she talks out loud,
She moves her hand, she shakes her head and laughs.
Is this mechanical marvel to be mine?
Quite paralyzed, I nod and nod and nod
And smile and smile. The gin is getting low
In my tooth glass. The hour is getting on.
Gin and adrenalin finally rescue me
(With an assist from Sally) and I find
My lips saluting hers as if she were
My stern commanding officer. No fool,
She puts us on an equal footing. Soon
My strategies and tactics are as toys
Before the gallop of her cavalry
That tramples through my blood and captures me.

4. Five-Fifty

Later, as racy novels used to say,
Later, I turn to see the westering sun
Through the ailanthus stipple her tan side
With yellow coin dots shaped to fit her skin.
This Sally now does like a garment wear
The beauty of the evening; silent, bare,
Hips, shoulders, arms, tresses, and temples lie.
I watch her as she sleeps, the tapering back
Rising and falling on the tide of breath;
The long eyelashes lying on her cheek;
The black brows and the light mouth both at rest;
A living woman not a foot away.

The west wind noses in at the window,
Sending a scent of soap, a hint of her
Perfume, and the first onions of the night
Up the airshaft to where I lie, not quite alone.

II.

The Tree Warden

I. A Farewell to Elms

In late July, now, leaves begin to fall:
A wintry skittering on the summer road,
Beside which grass, still needing to be mowed,
Gives rise to Turk's-caps, whose green tapering ball-
Point pens all suddenly write red. Last year,
The oriole swung his nest from the high fan
Vault of our tallest elm. Now a tree man
Tacks quarantine upon its trunk. I hear

An orange note a long way off, and thin
On our hill rain the ochre leaves. The white
Age of a weathered shingle stripes the bark.
Now surgeons sweat in many a paling park
And bone saws stammer blue smoke as they bite
Into the height of summer. Fall, begin.

II. The Second Equinox

Perambulating his green wards, the tree
Warden sees summer's ashes turn to fall:
The topmost reaches first, then more, then all
The twigs take umbrage, publishing a sea

Of yellow leaflets as they go to ground.
Upon their pyres, the maples set red stars,
The seal of sickness unto death that bars
The door of summer. Bare above its mound

Of leaves, each tree makes a memorial
To its quick season and its sudden dead;
With a whole gale of sighs and heaving head,
Each ash attends its annual burial.

The warden, under a boreal blue sky,
Reminds himself that ashes never die.

III. December Thirty-first

The days drew in this fall with infinite art,
Making minutely earlier the stroke
Of night each evening, muting what awoke
Us later every morning: the red heart

Of sun. December's miniature day
Is borne out on its stretcher to be hung,
Dim, minor, and derivative, among
Great august canvases now locked away.

Opposed to dated day, the modern moon
Comes up to demonstrate its graphic skill:
Laying its white-on-white on with a will,
Its backward prism makes a monotone.

In the New Year, night after night will wane;
Color will conquer; art will be long again.

IV. May Day

Help me. I cannot apprehend the green
Haze that lights really upon the young
Aspens in our small swamp, but not for long.
Soon round leaves, as a matter of routine,
Will make their spheric music; and too soon
The stunning green will be a common place.
Sensational today runs in our race
To flee the might of May for willing June.

To reach a bunch of rusty maple keys,
Undoing a world of constants, more or less,
I tread on innocence. The warden sees
In May Day the historical success
Of labor; a safe date for planting trees;
A universal signal of distress.

Our Literary Heritage

I. RIVERSIDE DRIVE, 1929

"'Good-by, Ralph. It should end some other way.
Not this,' Corinna said. 'Now go away.'
No. Rhymes. It's ludicrous. Try 'Dear, good-by.'
No. Repetitious. Maybe 'Dear, farewell.'
No. Stagy. Out of character. Oh, hell.
Time for a drink." The Smith-Corona heaves
As he retracts his knickerbockered knees
To rise. Outside, a southbound tug receives
The sun broadside, and the bold Linit sign
Pales on the Jersey shore. Fresh gin, tk-tk-
Tk-tk-tk-tk, quite clearly fills his glass
Half full from the unlabelled bottle. Now
His boyish fingers grip the siphon's worn
Wire basketweave and press the trigger down
To utter soda water. One long sip
Subtracts a third of it for carrying.
On the way back, he pauses at the door
Beside his football picture, where a snore
Attests that all is well and promises
Him time to work. To work: before the tall,
Black, idle typewriter, before the small
Black type elitely inching on the blank
White sea of bond, he quails and takes a drink.
First, demolitions: the slant shilling mark

Defaces half a hundred characters
With killing strike-overs. Now, a new start:
"'Good-by, Ralph. I don't know why it should end
Like tihs,' Corinna said. 'But be my freind.'"

II. Hotel Shawmut, Boston, 1946

(From a commercial travellers' hotel,
Professor S. jumped straight down into hell,
While—jug-o'-rum-rum—engines made their way
Beneath him, one so cold December day.)

While he prepares his body, cold gears mate
And chuckle in the long draught of the street.
He shaves; his silver spectacles peruse
An issue of *The North American Muse.*
He uses Mum; outside him in the hall,
Maids talk their language; snow begins to fall.
He puts on his old clothes. The narrow room
Has nothing, nothing to discuss with him
Except what time you should send out your suit
And shoes for cleaning. Now he stamps his foot:
Outside the window, not saying anything,
Appears a seagull, standing on one wing;
A long-awaited colleague. With glad cry,
Professor S. embraces the white sky.

While S. demolishes a taxicab,
His spectacles review the life of Crabbe.

(From a commercial travellers' hotel,
Professor S. descended into hell.
But once in April in New Haven he
Kissed a friend's sister in the gloom of trees.)

III. Deus Ex Machina, Flushing, 1966

La Guardia. Knee-deep in storyboards,
I line up for the shuttle, which arrives
Outside the gate and off-loads shuffling streams
Of transferees—each in his uniform
Of sober stuff and nonsense, with a case
Of talents at his side—who pass our line
Of sombre-suited shuttlers carrying
Our cases on. Then one appears, a rare
Bird in migration to New York, a bare-
Crowned singer of the stony coast of Maine,
And of Third Avenue in rain; a bard.
The way of the almost-extinct is hard.
He peers through tortoise-shelly glasses at
The crowd, the place, the year. He is not here
And is. In his check jacket, he describes
An arc of back and arms as he proceeds
Between two city starlings, carrying
His store of songs in a beat leather grip
And a dried drop of his brown lamb's blood on
His wilted collar. A *Time*-reader in
Glenurquhart plaid identifies his bird—
"Godwit, the poet"—to a flannel friend.
The bard stalks on on his two legs, aware
He has been spotted; in, I'd say, some pain
At an existence which anticipates
Its end and in the meantime tolerates
Intolerance of the wing, the whim, the one
Unanswerable voice which sings alone.

IV. Lament for the Makers, Including Me: 1967

New-minted coin, my poet's mask
(A small denomination in

Demotic nickel, brass, or tin)
Passes from hand to hand to hand
Beyond my six acres of land.
Did I desire such currency
Among the meritocracy
Of tri-named ladies who preserve
The flame of art in mackled hands,
Of universitarians
And decimal librarians
Who shore and store up textual
Addenda, of asexual
Old arbiters and referees
Who startle letters with a sneeze,
Of critics whose incautious cough
Halts a new wave or sends it off
To break on uninhabited shores,
Of publishers, insensual bores
Procuring art—"A maidenhead!"—
To Jack the Reader, of well-read
Young underfaced admirers who
Impinge on undefended you
At readings in all colleges?
No, I did not; but knowledge is
All-powerless to seek redress
For injuries to innocence.
I think continually of
Abjurers, who, fed on self-love,
Housed in an incommodious cave,
Clothed in three-button sackcloth, crave
Indulgence of no audience
But their own laudatory ears.
Alack, this anchoritic few
Dwindles; these ticking times are too
Struck with celebrity's arrears,
And heap past-due advances on
The embryonic artisan;
All hours from dawn to night are lauds,
All auditors are all applause

(However electronic), all
Tempters conspire in Adam's fall.

The world turned upside-down, without
A beast in view, without a doubt,
Recalls its exiles and bestows
On them the palm, the bays, the rose
(Art sick?), the Laurel Wormser Prize,
Whose debased dollar only buys
More nods, more goods, more fame, more praise:
Not art, as in the rude old days.

Now worldward poets turn and say,
Timor vitae conturbat me.

Just a Whack at Empson

We rot and rot and rot and rot and rot.
Why not cut badinages to the bone?
Alas, cockchafers cuddle. We cannot.

We recognise the hand upon our twat;
Unfortunately X is always known.
We rot and rot and'rot and rot and rot.

Unfortunately X is always not
Quite what we had in mind to end our moan.
Alas, cockchafers cuddle. We cannot.

Why must we be contained within our pot
Of message which we have so long outgrown?
We rot and rot and rot and rot and rot.

Your physic beauty made my inwards hot
Whilst talking to you on the telephone.
Alas, cockchafers cuddle. We cannot.

Each greening apple has its browning spot:
"The rank of every poet is well-known."
We rot and rot and rot and rot and rot.
Alas, cockchafers cuddle. We cannot.

Dear George Orwell, 1950–1965

Dear George Orwell,
I never said farewell.
There was too much going on:
Crabgrass in the lawn
And guests to entertain,
Light bantering with pain
(But wait till later on),
Love nightly come and gone.
But always in the chinks
Of my time (or the bank's),
I read your books again.
In Schrafft's or on the run
To my demanding clients,
I read you in the silence
Of the spell you spun.
My dearest Englishman,
My stubborn unmet friend,
Who waited for the end
In perfect pain and love
And walked to his own grave
With a warm wink and wave
To all; who would not pull
The trigger on the bull
Elephant, and who,
Seeing his foe undo
His pants across the lines,

Did not blow out his brains;
Who served the Hôtel X
As low man, slept in spikes
With tramps, in Rowton Houses
With pavement artists, boozers,
Boys, insomniacs;
Who spat on shams and hacks,
Lived in a raddled flat
Passing trains hooted at,
And died for what we are.
Farewell, Eric Blair.

Peace Comes to Still River, Mass.

Down at Fort Devens guns begin again:
I hear the thirties rattle, and the thin
Patter of rifles, each manned by a man
Invisible, disposable, and in
Our first line of defense, the paper says.
Now howitzers inflame our darkling days,
Exclaiming downrange in an O of fire
Upon their targets, and a virid flare
Gives the high sign to go on making war
In earnest of our inner truce. Once more
My quondam dean in University Hall
Stands in the breach of peace, whence he will call
Down fire on the bald, woolly heads of all
Professors of the other point of view,
Who, flanked and enfiladed and too few,
Will soon throw down their dated arms, of course,
And yield themselves to a superior force
Of well-drilled intellectual police,
Sworn on our honor to enforce the peace.

The Marschallin, Joy Street, July 3, 1949

> Manchmal hör' ich sie fliessen—
> unaufhaltsam.
> Manchmal steh' ich auf mitten in der Nacht
> und lass die Uhren alle, alle stehn.
>
> —*Hofmannsthal,* Rosenkavalier

> The penal gaol of Mountjoy, gaol 'em and joy.
>
> —*James Joyce*

1.

At 2200 hours, a silver flare
Profusely illustrates the western air,
Sending poor Mona Mountjoy to the heights
Of her tall town house overlooking Joy
And Pinckney Streets. Her long and shapely brown
Hands, dusted with the first faint liver spots
As if by accident, pick up her husband's Zeiss
Night glasses and range in on Harvard Square,
Bearing 290 at ten thousand yards.
Fire one! A small white integer appears,
Bears a huge school of yellow pollywogs,
And, with a white wink, vanishes. The boom
Takes twenty-seven seconds to arrive
Across East Cambridge as the crow flies. Now
A star shell bursts northeast. Dim in the south,
Dorchester Heights replies, and at her feet
The Common coughs up its first rocket of the night,
A red stem blooming in an amber star,
Which splits (by fission) into asterisks
As numerous and green as grass. At last
Her Major General has gone west tonight
(Though only literally), riding in a Jeep
Like any of his boys, and soon will sleep
Or lie, not unaccompanied, in the red
Light of a motel sign in Plattsburgh, where
He bivouacs for the morning march to Drum.

2.

The Major General is gone; alas,
Without replacement. Ian Quinn tonight
Is racing for Bermuda in the moon
Which rises earlier for seafarers
Bound east. Northwest, an imitation moon
Sails over Cambridge and divides itself
Impartially in seven satellites
White as the Pleiades. A Common sun
Rim-lights her long face with its Sayward nose
And dark-blue Dunster eyes. A river wind
Stirs her half-silver hair, switches her dress
Around her knees, whistles a winter air
Among the guy wires. Dimly, deep downstairs,
A doorbell rings beneath the rocketry,
And Anna goes to answer. At this hour
Who would walk up the steep side of Joy Street
To call on her? Bad news? A telegram?
A yellow pang? No, now they use the 'phone.
She steps into the black trap to the top
Story, her long legs in up to the knee;
Then she is a tall torso, and then she
Takes her blond disembodied head below.
The dark fifth-story boxroom is still hot.
A fan croons in the maid's room on the fourth.
Her own third-floor bedroom is dark and still.
The upstairs parlor is lit by one lamp.
The downstairs one contains her husband's Uncle Will.

3.

Returning, he says (over a long Scotch
Which he has made himself, apparently),
Returning from a meeting at the Union Club
Of the Parnassian Sodality
(Where, with his classmates of the Class of '94,

He sang, "Drink to Me Only with Thine Eyes,"
"We'll Go No More A-Roving," and, to close,
"Fair Harvard," in his obbligato voice);
Returning across Beacon and up Joy
Toward his little flat in Myrtle Street,
He thought to stop and call upon his niece,
And tell her his good news. (Out of one eye
She spies his dog-eared yellow calling card
On Anna's silver tray.) Good news indeed:
Will has determined to become betrothed,
At last, at last, to a lady of family.
One Mona knows; a famous beauty; young.
(He punctuates his points with a gold cane.)
In fact, Will says, his trustee's voice a thread
Of cunning whispering out of his starred face:
In fact, he is effecting nothing less
Than one more union of the Mountjoy line
With, — yes, the Saywards. Here is her picture,
Which a few hours ago at a rendezvous
She pressed into his hand; her miniature.
Mona takes the smudged half-column cut
Clipped from this morning's *Herald* society page.
"Post-deb," it says, "assists at fashion tea."
The girl is Sally Sayward, her own niece.
His eyes as blue as starry chicory flowers
In vacant lots, his purple smile as warm
As summertime, his manners beautiful
As any plate in *Godey's Lady's Book,*
He rises now to take his leave. "Enough,
My dear, of my good news. I must be off.
Good night, good night." Above Will's trilby hat,
The roof of Pinckney Street is shot with fire.

4.

The fireworks are not done. She goes upstairs
To her housetop again. A grunt of rain

Clouds in the west announces the intent
Of the deluge to fall on schedule,
As promised on the radio. The Park
Commissioners of Cambridge show at last
The color of their money in a green,
Red, azure, nude, cerise, and chartreuse blast,
Whose elegant ballistics shame the moon.
Its third stage, firing, adumbrates the flank
Of the first nimbus cloud, whose sheer freeboard
Goes straight up twenty-seven thousand feet,
Past cumulus to cirrus. She remarks
The coolness of its first forerunning winds,
Their spearheads bypassing strong points of heat.
On such a night she met the General,
Disguised as Minot Mountjoy, bond broker,
Concealing the identity of the head
Of Hall & Mountjoy; equally disguised
As Captain Mountjoy of the 26th,
Whose olive shoulderboards sustained the pips
Which would grow into the commanding stars
Of 26th Division, National Guard,
Through the good offices of thirty years.
On such a night in 1922,
She met Mountjoy in summer's high estate,
An awkward Sayward daughter now a swan,
A beauty, twenty, and imprisoned him
With her short blond bob and her long dark laugh,
As he imprisoned her in the high place
She occupies alone on Joy Street now.

5.

Someplace, apparently Arlington, begins
Its own fire fight in the northwest. On such
A night, too, she met Ian Quinn. In June,
The Eastern Yacht Club is lit up at night
With amber lanterns where the members dance

Indoors and out; there, just two years ago,
She first danced with him. In the low light, she
Carried her forty-five years well; and he,
Worn with ten years at sea and four at war,
Looked older than his thirty-three. Two years,
Two years now they have occupied plotting
To intersect their courses on a chart
Awash with obstacles: stubborn routines
Running abysmally deep; mutual friends
Marking their channel everywhere like rocks;
Exhausting care and caution forming bars
To their resolve. (Against this set the shock
Of his hands on her bare arms in the dark
Hotel room after a month's absence, or
The quick kiss—"Watch my lipstick!"—at her door,
Containing a month's worth of intimacy.)
Nevertheless, the end is perfectly clear.

6.

Its magazines hit by a lucky shot,
The first cloud bursts into internal fire,
Suddenly started, suddenly put out.
When will his skillful, luckless shot hit her?
Soon. Only this morning, in her hand mirror,
She read between the lines state's evidence
Amassed by forty-seven years. No doubt
She dreamt again last night of waking in the small
Of the night's back and stopping all the clocks,
Upstairs and down, because she could not bear
To hear time running through its tidemarks. All
The signs are negative; the hour glass drops
To storm point; still the thunderheads come on.

7.

The Common finishes its business
For one more year with an immense barrage

Of small white rockets with a terrier's sharp
And penetrating bark. In the bright lights
Of their impermanent sky sign can be seen
One tear in her eye, to memorialize
The fact that one day, now, tomorrow, or
Next year, he will leave her for someone else
Younger and prettier, as her glass predicts.
Stupid to speculate: but if she had
Her wrenching wish, it would be Sally Sayward,
Her gawky niece irradiating love,
Her silly self at twenty over again.

    8.

Before its time, chain lightning makes next day
Out of tonight, then fuses all its lights
With a white snick and a black avalanche,
Burying here and now and far away.
So time utters an annual report,
Heard loud and clear, on its last fiscal year
In the man market, on its day-to-day
Quotations, on its gains in brick and clay,
Its wins on the Exchange and in the Court
Of No Resort. The last man-made stars burn
Out in the west, the last spectacular
Dwindles to darkness in the captured fort.
The dandelions of light now go to seed.
In Joy Street, Mona Mountjoy, like the year,
Ends her summation and begins to turn
Toward the dockets of more pressing need:
A house to keep, a failure to hold dear,
A fiction to maintain, another year
To fill with guest appearances, each day
Farced full, penned black and blue, marked with a mort
Of dates, engagements, living tongues to learn
At Berlitz, trips to take, and friends to mourn.
Being herself, she takes it well indeed;
She has had all the fireworks she will need.

She goes belowstairs, an unbroken reed,
To put her windows down against the rain.

Sondra Dead or Alive

I. CAMBRIDGE, 1955

The trouble was nobody laughed at her
Too witty poems when she read in 5
Harvard Hall. Professor Dix was there.
He smiled. Hardly a man is now alive.

Nevertheless, she is the talk of the town.
Or gown, at least. Divinity Avenue
Is bathed in her florescence. Down around
Memorial Drive she is a *succès fou*.

In her garden last night I laughed. Alas, too late.
I am afraid it came in the wrong place.
A poetess defends her puny kit
Fiercer than tigresses. Witness my face.

How can we classify this astonishing piece
Of resistance? Her underground effrontery
Is now quite superficial; underneath
The loud whalebone she is a quiet country.

Perhaps. Sumner, her husband, does not say
Word one. Burdened, he sometimes sighs.
Transfixed by his prize catch, day after day
He eats her with his macroscopic eyes.

II. LE TOMBEAU DE SONDRA MANN

Outside the Ritz, half-past our fifth Martini
With a twist I hand you into your Healey,

Returning your spirituous kiss, not really
Caught in your gin as you turn up Newbury.

The blat of your exhaust scatters the leaves
Of a December *Herald* underfoot;
For halt pedestrians you give a hoot
And pop the clutch in potently, O brave

And disappearing racer, all too soon
Vanished beyond the end of Berkeley Street.
Now, queen and huntress in a bucket seat,
How come I pace your grave in the new moon?

ENVOY

As I sat in the Ritz-Carlton, drinking the crystal wine,
And outside in the world the old moon died, a silver rind,
They told me you were dead, chauffeur, and I, for auld lang syne,
Took one more cup of kindness for the coldness that was mine.

Man and Wife

You were a unit when I saw you last:
The handsome husband and the happy wife,
Which was an act; but tissue of the past
Between you, unseen, made you one for life,

Or so I thought. It seems that I was wrong.
Seeing you ten years later, the kids grown
And gone, the still light of the long
Living room coming between you, I should have known

The lines were down. Your life went on with such
Attention to unchange: each "darling" fell

With metered carelessness; each "please" with much
Conviction; each "thanks" rang true as a bell.

But when you walked me to the door to go,
I saw the fault between your faces. Oh.

Two Happenings in Boston

I. A Disappearance in West Cedar Street

Did Shriner die or make it to New York?
In his side room, across the hall from mine,
Wide windows air bare ticking. On a line
Outside, clean sheets flap. Samples of his work

Litter the closet: a barbed, wiry nude
In his hirsute pen line; a sketch of me
In ink and wash; a torn gouache of three
Pears on a windowsill. A cache of food —

Saltines, Velveeta Cheese, dried apricots —
Hid in a cairn of bags is now laid bare.
Also a bathrobe belt, one sock, a pair
Of sneakers with frayed laces tied in knots,

A paperback "Candide." Did Shriner die
While I was on the Cape? Did his cough stop
Dead in the welfare ward? Did a blue cop
Wheel Shriner out under the summer sky?

Did absolutely nobody appear
When they interred his box in Potter's Field?
(*I* would have been there.) Did nobody yield
A summer hat, a winter thought, a tear?

Or did he make it to New York? Did his
Ship dock at last at Fifty-seventh Street?
Did angels, agents, and collectors meet
His price for life? Is that where Shriner is?

Does he sit down now in Minetta's late
With mistresses and models on each hand?
And is he now an icon in the land
Of mind and matter southward of Hell Gate?

Grey curtains flutter. A tall smell of pork
Ascends the stairs. The landlady below
Tells me in broken English she don't know.
Did Shriner die or make it to New York?

II. A Reading in Huntington Avenue

Hernando Milton, scion of the grey
Daylight that realizes all the stale
Unprofitable flats of the Fenway,
Halftone from head to foot, beyond the pale

Of ordinary people, reads his play
Aloud in the Alliance of the Arts,
Heard out by the dried flower of the Back Bay,
In moulting foxes, as he takes all parts.

That phalanx of once-marbled womanhood
Whose forties closed their minds and shut their hearts
Adores to hear the son of the late good
Nan Makepeace, sadly laid low by the darts

Of two degenerative diseases; lewd
Behavior by her disappearing husband, missed
Alone by whisperers; extremely rude
News of her son; and one obituarist.

Hernando Makepeace Milton, known as Nan
(Just like his mother) to a little list
Of boys on Beacon Hill, reads with élan
To the foxed ladies who will miss the gist,

With luck, of his verse play, entitled "Pan
And Hemp," and wholly dedicated to
The keen sensations of a happy man
(Himself) while smoking hashish. No one who

Savors the sound of words like a devotee
Of the Alliance of the Arts dares do
More than lie back and let a lurid sea
Of tone colors ravish her hair-do.

The baby-blue spot points to the last dance
Spun out by Milton, whose whole face is blue
With that light and the onset of a trance
Of *cannabis indica*. The play comes true.

The West Forties: Morning, Noon, and Night

But nothing whatever is by love debarred.
—*Patrick Kavanagh*

I. Welcome to Hotel Majesty (Singles $4 Up)

On this hotel, their rumpled royalties
Descend from their cross-country busses, loyalties
Suspended, losses cut, loves left behind,
To strike it lucky in the state of mind
That manufactures marvels out of mud.
Ensanguined by a bar sign selling Bud,
The early-streamline lobby—in its shell

Of late-Edwardian ornament, with a bell-
Mouthed cupidon extolling every swag
On its tall, fruitful front (a stale sight gag
First uttered by the comic landsmen who
Compounded a Great White Way out of blue
Sky, gneiss, and schist a whole stone age ago,
Before time steeled the arteries we know)——
The lobby washes redly over guests
With rope-bound bags containing their one best
Suit, shirt, tie, Jockey shorts, and pair of socks,
Half-empty pint, electric-razor box,
Ex-wife's still-smiling picture, high-school ring,
Harmonica, discharge, and everything.
Amid the alien corn and ruthless tares,
I hear a royal cry of horseplayers
Winding their tin horns in a chant of brass,
Their voices claiming in the wilderness.

II. Sal's Atomic Submarines

The Puerto Rican busboy, Jesus, coughs
Above the cutting board where Sal compiles
An outbound order for the Abinger
Associates next door; then, carrying
A pantheon of Heroes in a brown
Kraft-paper bag, he slides by the chrome-
Formica-plastic dinette furniture
And gains the world, where anti-personnel
Gasses from crosstown busses, vegetable
Soup simmering at Bickford's, and My Sin
Seeping from Walgreen's silently combine
To addle all outsiders. Only lithe,
Quick indigenes like Jesus (whose tan neck
Is thinner than my wrist) can long survive
And later even prosper in the air
Of these times' squares, these hexahedral hives
Where every worker bustles for his Queen.

III. Penny Arcadia

Like lava, rock erupts to fill the room
From each coäx-, coäx-, coäxial
Concentric speaker's throat, and rolls like doom
Over the unmoved pinball-playing boys,
Whose jaws lightly reciprocate like long-
Stroke pistons coupled to the Tinguely loom
Of augmented electric music, strong
As sexuality and loud as noise,
Which keens across the dingy room at full
Gain, and, its coin gone, as abruptly dies.

IV. Stage Door Johnny's

Silvana Casamassima, Vic Blad
(The talent agent), Lance Bartholomey,
Piretta Paul, Max Dove, A. Lincoln Brown,
Samarra Brown, Lil Yeovil, Beryl Cohn
(Theatrical attorney), Johnny Groen
(The owner), Merritt Praed, Morty Monroe,
Dame Phyllis Woolwich, Sir Jack Handel, Bart.,
Del Specter (the producer), Coquetel,
Fab Newcomb, Temple Bell, Vanessa Vane,
Burt Wartman, C. R. Freedley, F.R.S.,
Alf Wandsworth (author of "Queer Street"), Mel Hess,
His Honor Judge Perutz, Merced McCall,
Tam Pierce, Bill Brewer, Tom Cobley, and all
The darlings, mirrored in their flourishing
Autographed caricatures on every wall,
Sail on, sealed in, important, bright, serene,
In league in Captain Nemo's submarine.

V. M. Wax Loans

Clear and obscure, elbows of saxophones
Shine out like sink traps in an underworld
Of pledges unredeemed: a spectral band
Of brass and nickel marching in the dark

Toward the morning and redemption, where
Known lips will kiss their reeds, familiar hands
Resume their old and loving fingering.
Unlikely: in a hundred rented rooms
From here to Ybor City, pledgors plan
What next to pawn: the Rolleicord, the ring,
The eight-transistor Victor radio,
The travelling alarm. Alarm creeps in-
To all their calculations, now the bloom
Is off their promise, now the honeymoon
Is over with a cry, and time begins
To whittle expectations to a size
Convenient for their carrying to pawn.

VI. LOVEMOVIE

Before the glazed chrome case where Lovelies Swim
Au Natural, and under the sly lights
Which wink and bump and wink and grind, except
For those that have burnt out, the singing strings
Of Madame Violin essay "Caprice,"
Not missing many notes, considering
How cold it is outside the Lovemovie.
Stray pennies in her tin cup punctuate
The music like applause. Play, gypsies! Dance!
The thin strains of a Romany romance
Undaunt the ears of each peajacketed
Seaman on liberty, and of each old
Wanderer slowly losing to the cold,
And of each schoolboy who has come to see
Life in the flesh inside the Lovemovie.
Beneath her stiff green hair, an artist's grin
Knits up the ravelled cheek of Madame Violin.

VII. THE ARGO BUILDING: NEW DELMAN'S GOOD NIGHT

The last bone button in the old tin tea
Box of the Argo Building lastly sees

GNIVAEWER ELBISIVNI peeling off
His street-side window as he locks the door
Of 720 one more night, and struts
His septuagenarian stuff down
The corridor, past Aabco Dental Labs,
Worldwide Investigations, Inc., Madame
Lillé, Corsetiere, Star School of Tap,
Dr. O'Keefe, Franck Woodwind Institute,
Wink Publications, and Watch Hospital.
Up the wrought shaft, preceded by its wires
Ticking and twittering, the intrepid car
Rises like an old aeronaut to take
Its ballast-passenger aboard beneath
The pointed clear bulbs of its four flambeaux,
Sweetly attenuated art nouveau
Which was *vieux jeu* and is the rage, unknown
To old New Delman, whom it ferries down
In its black cage, funebrially slow,
To Stygian Forty-seventh Street below.

The Nanny Boat, 1957

> Towards the end he sailed into an extraordinary mildness,
> And anchored in his home and reached his wife
> And rode within the harbour of her hand . . .
>
> — *W. H. Auden*

> Relish the love of a gentle woman.
> — *John Cheever*

I. DOWN

1.

A surf of people, backlit by the sun,
Washes across Atlantic Avenue

To Rowe's Wharf, where the Nanny Boat awaits
Its gilt-edged Friday-night commuters, borne
Out of the city on a roasting wave
Of Victor Coffee. Soon that city scent
Gives in to those of shore and sea. You step
Infinitely daintily, treading my heart
With your white size-five foot, aboard the boat
Bound for Nantasket and for night, where you
Will understudy seas in undulant
Compliance and reception, swamping all
My longboat adjectives. Cast off the bow
And stern lines linking us to the upright,
August, and sobersided city, and
Back half-speed out into the glassy reach —
Cased yellow by the molten sun — which leads
South to anonymous liberties, where town
Clothes come ungirt and naked bankers lie
Late on the sand beside associates.

  2.

My Nikon neatly juxtaposes you,
Tall, dominant, with the recessive, squat
Skyline of Boston, in its unabridged
Wide-angle condensation. Click, and it
Is history, distorted, black-and-white,
And two-dimensional at that. (Think now,
Eight good years later, of those passages
To sea and not to sea, those passages
Between us which we shared with Spectacle
Island and Gallup's Island, those long green
Fluent quotations of cold fact and salt
Occurrences about the boat, which, aureous,
For the short span of sunset, blanched and went blue
When day was done.) Later, the running lights,
The dusty bulbs above the bar, the cream
Fluorescent strips refract on the night air

And make a great white, green, red, cream
Mirage on the horizon, even beyond
Hull Gut and Bumpkin Island. The Sturgeon Moon
Levers itself, yellow as piano keys,
Out of the eastern sea and stains the waves
Its summer color. Lovers, limited,
Perhaps, to this boat ride to demonstrate
Their aims, melt into one under the moon
Along the promenade deck; we, sedate,
Smoke, knowing we can well afford to wait
For spring tides in the middle of the night.

II. THERE

1.

The far mirage is an oasis now: .
Beyond World's End, the spitting negative
Image of the city we left at five
Takes shape in the solutions of the sea.
Black towers go white, and, shivering to the shore,
Lead our wide eyes up white towers in the air
Above the sky signs advertising love
In a lost language: O's of ferris wheels,
The cursive of the roller coaster, scrawls
Of neon on the rooflines of dance halls,
All ciphers for a scholar to decode.
Your face, a spectrogram, reflects their shades
Of meaning, green, red, white, as we slip in
To dock at this free port of noise, whose din—
Calliopes, pop records, human cries—
Projects the same sensational offer of
Love for mere money, though the easy terms
Are unintelligible through
The language barrier, *comprenez-vous?*
But on the dock, spelled out in silver light
Dispensed by Paragon Park, we read two old

Familiar names, Frannie and Ed, who wait
In the old yellow Willys wagon. Friends,
Greet two new voyagers to the World's End.

2.

Out those wide windows Hingham paints itself,
Impeccably, if academically,
In the low-key, representational
Shades of a summer night. Well to the west,
A knot of lights, the Center, sends a line
In Morse across the water to Crow Point,
Calling my maritime interests to
Three granite islets, possibly archly named
Ragged, Sarah, Langlee, harboring
Just underneath my window. The moon's sway
As night-light laureate is threatened by
Arc lightning in the western front of cloud.
My host's voice calls me back. I wake and drown
In the dry world of letters. "Lefty, you
Don't really mean it about Gilbert, do
You, seriously, I mean?" "Why, sure I do,"
I say. "Come on, just tell me who
Else wrote a decent line of satire in
The bloody century. Why, Porter and
The Major-General are radical
Caricatures, Ed, archetypes." "Go *on!*"
"No really." "Hell, let's have a nightcap." "Yeah!"
We toast our differences in B.P.R.
And Pierce's No. 6 commingled. Wug!
That's bracing going down. The evening ends
In inconclusion, as it should with friends.

3.

To quote my later self, "I punctuate
Your long body with exclamations." Not
Terribly temperate; nor was I then,

Between a skinful of cheap rye and a
Head full of Great Ideas. Then there was you
To blame, with that invisible smirk
I could see as plain as anything in the dark,
And your slow pulse just slipping up the shore
And barely sliding back, and worst of all,
Your cool electrifying skin humming
With wattage waiting for the switch to close.
Fused and short-circuited at last, we doze
Until a jovial thunderclap hits home
And takes our pictures with a massive flash
That just goes on and on, while we sit up
Like couples caught by eyes in hotel rooms,
And face the music. Rain comes down like doom.

III. BACK

1.

A bodkin through my head, I watch the view,
Which, as a dayscape, paints itself anew
(With cunning strokes around the shoreline), while
I wait for bacon frying. Mesmerized
By smoke from your bent Viceroy, you still sit
Cross-legged on the sofa, eyes at ease.
Soon we will fly from this well-ordered here,
Complete with friends, to an amorphous there,
Hull down on the horizon, where we will
Take steps to walk together or apart.
Whichever, in this moment I concede
Your beauty and necessity aside
From any need of mine, which makes my need
Decided and imperative. Be mine.

2.

Pink stucco steams behind us as we steam
Away from hot Nantasket, where the brass
Poles of the carrousels, the steering wheels
Of Dodg'ems, and the rusty grab rails on
The front of roller-coaster cars are all
Too hot to touch, and where the towering
Totems of Popeye, Jiggs, and Mickey Mouse
(Done by some village Lichtenstein, some mute
Inglorious Warhol using old house paint)
Peel in the August sun, while we creep in
To the tiny shade of the top deck, drinking
Warm, sticky Coke in paper cups. They pass,
The harbor islands, one by one, astern,
Rapt in a heat haze. The sleek, moneyed sea,
All gold and green, turns in its figured sheets
As it sleeps off a stormy night. We draw
The city slowly closer to our bow.

3.

All this our north stinks peace. The cabbage leaves
Downtrodden on the Market cobbles, and
The fish heads festering in garbage cans
Outside the shuttered fish stores lend their loud
Saturday odors to disturb the peace
Of Sunday in the city. Carrying
Your Winship overnight bag, I walk up
The shady side of every street beside
You, to the desert waste of Cambridge Street.
We brave the sun to cross. Around the bend
Under the El, and up West Cedar Street,
And up four flights to your apartment, where
You turn the fan on, and I'm home
At last with you the first time in my life,
My anchor, my harbor, my second wife.

Love-Making; April; Middle Age

A fresh west wind from water-colored clouds
Stirs squills and iris shoots across the grass
Now turning fiery green. This storm will pass
In dits and stipples on the windowpane
Where we lie high and dry, and the low sun
Will throw rose rays at our grey heads upon
The back-room bed's white pillows. Venus will
Descend, blue-white, in horizontal airs
Of red, orange, ochre, lemon, apple green,
Cerulean, azure, ultramarine,
Ink, navy, indigo, at last midnight.
Now, though, this clouded pewter afternoon
Blurs in our window and intensifies
The light that dusts your eyes and mine with age.

We turn our thirties over like a page.

Dying: An Introduction

Always too eager for future, we
Pick up bad habits of expectancy.
—*Philip Larkin*

I. RING AND WALK IN

Summer still plays across the street,
An ad-hoc band
In red, white, blue, and green
Old uniforms
And borrowed instruments;
Fall fills the street
From shore to shore with leaves,
A jaundiced mass

Movement against the cold;
I slip on ice
Slicks under powder snow and stamp my feet
Upon the doctor's rubber mat,
Ring and Walk In
To Dr. Sharon's waiting room,
For once with an appointment,
To nonplus
Ugly Miss Erberus.
Across from other candidates —
A blue-rinsed dam
In Davidows, a husk
Of an old man,
A one-eyed boy — I sit
And share their pervigilium.
One *Punch* and two
Times later comes the call.

II. PROBABLY NOTHING

Head cocked like Art, the *Crimson* linotype
Operator, Dr. Sharon plays
Taps on my game leg, spelling out the name,
With his palpating fingers, of my pain.
The letters he types are not visible
To him or me; back up the melting pot
Of the machine, the matrix dents the hot
Lead with a letter and another: soon a word,
Tinkling and cooling, silver, will descend
To be imposed upon my record in
Black-looking ink. "My boy, I think," he says,
In the most masterly of schoolish ways,
In the most quiet of all trumps in A
Flat, "this lump is probably nothing, but" —
A but, a buzz of omen resonates —
"I'd check it anyway. Let's see when I
Can take a specimen." Quiet business

With the black phone's bright buttons. St, ssst, sst.
An inside call. In coded whispers. Over. Out.
"Can you come Friday noon? We'll do it then."
I nod I can and pass the world of men
In waiting, one *Life* farther on.

III. O.P.O.R.

Undressing in the locker room
Like any high school's, full of shades
In jockstraps and the smell of steam,
Which comes, I guess, from autoclaves,
And not from showers, I am struck
By the immutability,
The long, unchanging, childish look
Of my pale legs propped under me,
Which, nonetheless, now harbor my
Nemesis, or, conceivably,
Do not. My narcissistic eye
Is intercepted deftly by
A square nurse in a gas-green gown
And aqua mask — a dodo's beak —
Who hands me a suit to put on
In matching green, and for my feet
Two paper slippers, mantis green:
My invitation to the dance.
I shuffle to the table, where
A shining bank of instruments —
Service for twelve — awaits my flesh
To dine. Two nurses pull my pants
Down and start shaving. With a splash,
The Doctor stops his scrubbing-up
And walks in with a quiet "Hi."
Like hummingbirds, syringes tap
The novocaine and sting my thigh
To sleep, and the swordplay begins.
The stainless-modern knife digs in —

Meticulous trencherman — and twangs
A tendon faintly. Coward, I groan.
Soon he says "Sutures," and explains
To me he has his specimen
And will stitch up, with boundless pains,
Each severed layer, till again
He surfaces and sews with steel
Wire. "Stainless." Look how thin it is,
Held in his forceps. "It should heal
Without a mark." These verities
Escort me to the tiring room,
Where, as I dress, the Doctor says,
"We'll have an answer Monday noon."
I leave to live out my three days,
Reprieved from findings and their pain.

IV. PATH. REPORT

Bruisingly cradled in a Harvard chair
Whose orange arms cramp my pink ones, and whose black
Back stamps my back with splat marks, I receive
The brunt of the pathology report,
Bitingly couched in critical terms of my
Tissue of fabrications, which is bad.
That Tyrian specimen on the limelit stage
Surveyed by Dr. Cyclops, magnified
Countless diameters on its thick slide,
Turns out to end in -oma. "But be glad
These things are treatable today," I'm told.
"Why, fifteen years ago —" a dark and grave-
Shaped pause. "But now, a course of radiation, and —"
Sun rays break through. "And if you want X-ray,
You've come to the right place." A history,
A half-life of the hospital. Marie
Curie must have endowed it. Cyclotrons,
Like missile silos, lurk within its walls.
It's reassuring, anyway. But bland

And middle-classic as these environs are,
And sanguine as his measured words may be,
And soft his handshake, the webbed, inky hand
Locked on the sill, and the unshaven face
Biding outside the window still appall
Me as I leave the assignation place.

V. OUTBOUND

Outside, although November by the clock,
Has a thick smell of spring,
And everything—
The low clouds lit
Fluorescent green by city lights;
The molten, hissing stream
Of white car lights, cooling
To red and vanishing;
The leaves,
Still running from last summer, chattering
Across the pocked concrete;
The wind in trees;
The ones and twos,
The twos and threes
Of college girls,
Each shining in the dark,
Each carrying
A book or books,
Each laughing to her friend
At such a night in fall;
The two-and-twos
Of boys and girls who lean
Together in an A and softly walk
Slowly from lamp to lamp,
Alternatively lit
And nighted; Autumn Street,
Astonishingly named, a rivulet
Of asphalt twisting up and back

To some spring out of sight — and everything
Recalls one fall
Twenty-one years ago, when I,
A freshman, opening
A green door just across the river,
Found the source
Of spring in that warm night,
Surprised the force
That sent me on my way
And set me down
Today. Tonight. Through my
Invisible new veil
Of finity, I see
November's world—
Low scud, slick street, three giggling girls—
As, oddly, not as sombre
As December,
But as green
As anything:
As spring.

Canzone: Aubade

Morning, noon, afternoon, evening, and night
Are not all seasons that we need to know;
Though we would go lamely without the night,
Recircling on itself, night after night,
Assuring us an opposite, a way
To action of a kind that honest night
Would never dream of, sibilant brief night
Could not conceive: the bitter stroke of noon.
Better that we conceive of dawn than noon,
That place where all things shift, and middle night
Sits for its portrait in half light, and still
Sits obstinately in two lights, quite still.

Though dawn is at the window, you, all still,
Take the small part of small hours of the night
And sleep away the morning, small and still,
Till my minuscule action wakes you. Still,
I cannot think that you, awaking, know
The whispered confidence of nighttime still.
Outside, the city's streets are silent still;
And morning still attempts to find a way
To say itself; and donkey's years away
Keeps hot important midday, trying still
To blandish us with talk of afternoon;
But we know now the pitilessness of noon.

I cannot think of you at all at noon
As my late lover whose long body still
I punctuate with exclamations. Noon—
The rigid, brazen, upright arm of noon—
Casts a long shadow between now and night
Where intervened the tortuous forenoon:
The twice-told tale of snaillike afternoon,
That we know better than we need to know.
What is there, after all, for us to know
That meaning clings to in the eye of noon?
Through the slow afternoon we seek a way
Of meeting evening's sullen change halfway.

Now it is middle afternoon, halfway
To evening; and, looking back on noon,
I marvel to have found some kind of way
To pass the stolid hours that guard you. Way
Off somewhere in the darkness you lie still,
Not quite recapturable, and part way
To capturing you my thought falls away
To urgencies of afternoon. All night
Your phosphorescence clarifies the night,
Makes light of darkness, indicates the way
To tunnels' ending: darling, you must know
The dead-white end of the dark road we know.

New schemes, new modes, new paradigms? We know
All of our love must go the same old way.
We must discredit learning; all I know
Is evening keeping us apart. You know
Like me that memory at noon
Springs on us all the secrets that we know
About ourselves, to try if we can know
The agony of aloneness. Lying still,
We paint ourselves all black. O lover, still
It stirs me every evening to know
We pay such court to turnings in the night;
And my thoughts take you as if day were night.

ENVOY

At last, alas! day is born out of night,
And, though our pain persists in sleeping still,
It will arise and flourish at high noon,
And furious, constant, seek to find a way
Out of our time, the only one we know.

from

Scattered Returns

I.

A Deathplace

Very few people know where they will die,
But I do: in a brick-faced hospital,
Divided, not unlike Caesarean Gaul,
Into three parts: the Dean Memorial
Wing, in the classic cast of 1910,
Green-grated in unglazed, Aeolian
Embrasures; the Maud Wiggin Building, which
Commemorates a dog-jawed Boston bitch
Who fought the brass down to their whipcord knees
In World War I, and won enlisted men
Some decent hospitals, and, being rich,
Donated her own granite monument;
The Mandeville Pavilion, pink-brick tent
With marble piping, flying snapping flags
Above the entry where our bloody rags
Are rolled in to be sponged and sewn again.
Today is fair; tomorrow, scourging rain
(If only my own tears) will see me in
Those jaundiced and distempered corridors
Off which the five-foot-wide doors slowly close.
White as my skimpy chiton, I will cringe
Before the pinpoint of the least syringe;
Before the buttered catheter goes in;
Before the I.V.'s lisp and drip begins
Inside my skin; before the rubber hand

Upon the lancet takes aim and descends
To lay me open, and upon its thumb
Retracts the trouble, a malignant plum;
And finally, I'll quail before the hour
When the authorities shut off the power
In that vast hospital, and in my bed
I'll feel my blood go thin, go white, the red,
The rose all leached away, and I'll go dead.
Then will the business of life resume:
The muffled trolley wheeled into my room,
The off-white blanket blanking off my face,
The stealing, secret, private, *largo* race
Down halls and elevators to the place
I'll be consigned to for transshipment, cased
In artificial air and light: the ward
That's underground; the terminal; the morgue.
Then one fine day when all the smart flags flap,
A booted man in black with a peaked cap
Will call for me and troll me down the hall
And slot me into his black car. That's all.

Small Space

I

MEN PAST 40
GET UP NIGHTS
And look out at
City lights,
Wondering where they
Made the wrong
Turn, and why life
Is so long.

II

WOMAN NEARLY
ITCHED TO DEATH
As her body,
Filled with breath,
Tortured her with
Womanly
Longing, wholly
Humanly.

III

MAKES THESE THREE
MISTAKES IN SPEECH?
Hear them mermaids
On the beach
Singing real low
Each to each?
Had I ought to
Eat a peach?

Visiting Chaos

No matter how awful it is to be sitting in this
Terrible magazine office, and talking to this
Circular-saw-voiced West Side girl in a dirt-
Stiff Marimekko and lavender glasses, and this
Cake-bearded boy in short-rise Levi's, and hearing
The drip and rasp of their tones on the softening
Stone of my brain, and losing
The thread of their circular words, and looking
Out through their faces and soot on the window to
Winter in University Place, where a blue-
Faced man, made of rags and old newspapers, faces

A horrible grill, looking in at the food and the faces
It disappears into, and feeling,
Perhaps, for the first time in days, a hunger instead
Of a thirst; where two young girls in peacoats and hair
As long as your arm and snow-sanded sandals
Proceed to their hideout, a festering cold-water flat
Animated by roaches, where their lovers, loafing in wait
To warm and be warmed by brainless caresses,
Stake out a state
Of suspension; and where a black Cadillac 75
Stands by the curb to collect a collector of rents,
Its owner, the owner of numberless tenement flats;
And swivelling back
To the editorial pad
Of *Chaos,* a quarter-old quarterly of the arts,
And its brotherly, sisterly staff, told hardly apart
In their listlessly colorless sackcloth, their ash-colored skins,
Their resisterly sullenness, I suddenly think
That no matter how awful it is, it's better than it
Would be to be dead. But who can be sure about that?

Safety at Forty:
or, An Abecedarian Takes a Walk

Alfa is nice. Her Roman eye
Is outlined in an O of dark
Experience. She's thirty-nine.
Would it not be kind of fine
To take her quite aback, affront
Her forward manner, take her up
On it? Echo: of course it would.

Betta is nice. Her Aquiline
Nose prowly marches out between
Two raven wings of black sateen

Just touched, at thirty-five, with gray.
What if I riled her quiet mien
With an indecent, subterrene
Proposal? She might like me to.

Gemma is nice. Her Modenese
Zagato body, sprung on knees
As supple as steel coils, shocks
Me into plotting to acquire
The keys to her. She's twenty-nine.
Might I aspire to such a fine
Consort in middle age? Could be.

Della is nice. Calabrian
Suns engineered the sultry tan
Over (I'm guessing) all of her long
And filly frame. She's twenty-one.
Should I consider that she might
Look kindly on my graying hairs
And my too-youthful suit? Why not?

O Megan, all-American
Wife waiting by the hearth at home,
As handsome still at forty-five
As any temptress now alive,
Must I confess my weariness
At facing stringent mistresses
And head for haven? Here I come.

Solo, Head Tide

Far up the Sheepscot, where the tide goes out
And leaves the river water free of salt
And free to foster tame freshwater life
Far from the sea's tall terror, wave on wave

And tooth on tooth in the bone-handled jaws
Which ultramariners use as their laws,
I spy the first footprint of Robinson.
Though his birthplace gives little to go on,
He is implicit in the inward town
Where not a soul steps out of doors at noon
And no one stirs behind twelve-over-twelve
Panes in the windows. Walk uphill yourself
And stand before the shuttered clapboard church
Signed "1830" by its year of birth;
Look down through ash boughs on the whited town
Where they say he and his love slept alone
Under one roof for life, and where his moon
Singled him out, awake, each moonlight night
That spring tides steered upriver with their salt
And broke in these backwaters; feel his pulse
Still in the riverside and his strait house.

The Village: The Seasons

(To Saul Touster)

I. January 22, 1932

Could a four-year-old look out of a square sedan
(A Studebaker Six in currency green
With wooden artillery wheels) and see a scene
Of snow, light lavender, landing on deepening blue
Buildings built out of red-violet bricks, and black
Passersby passing by over the widening white
Streets darkening blue, under a thickening white
Sky suddenly undergoing sheer twilight,
And the yellow but whitening streetlights coming on,
And remember it now, though the likelihood is gone
That it ever happened at all, and the Village is gone

That it ever could happen in? Memory, guttering out,
Apparently, finally flares up and banishes doubt.

II. MAY 29, 1941

Tring. Bells
On grocers' boys' bicycles ring,
Followed, on cue,
By the jaunty one-note of prayers at two
Near churches; taxi horns, a-hunt,
Come in for treble; next, the tickety bass
Of chain-driven Diamond T's, gone elephantine
And stove-enamelled conifer green
Down Greenwich Avenue.
Out of the Earle
I issue at half-past thirteen,
Struck, like a floral clock,
By seasonal
Manifestations: unreasonable
N.Y.U. girls out in their bobby socks
And rayon blouses; meek boys with their books
Who have already moulted mackinaws;
Desarrolimiento of
New chrome-green leaves; a rose,
Got, blooming, out of bed; and Mrs. Roos-
Evelt and Sarah Delano
Descending the front stoop of a Jamesian
House facing south against the Square, the sun—
Who, curveting, his half course not yet run,
Infects the earth with crescence;
And the presence
Of process, seen in un-top-hatted,
Un-frock-coated burghers and their sons
And daughters, taking over
All title, right, and interest soever
In this, now their
Property, Washington Square.

III. DECEMBER 29, 1949

The Hotel Storia ascends
Above me and my new wife; ends
Eight stories of decline, despair,
Iron beds and hand-washed underwear
Above us and our leatherette
Chattels, still grounded on the wet
Grey tessellated lobby floor.
Soon, through a dingy, numbered door,
We'll enter into our new home,
Provincials in Imperial Rome
To seek their fortune, or, at least,
To find a job. The wedding feast,
Digested and metabolized,
Diminishes in idealized
Group photographs, and hard today
Shunts us together and at bay.
Outside the soot-webbed window, sleet
Scourges the vista of Eighth Street;
Inside, the radiators clack
And talk and tell us to go back
Where we came from. A lone pecan
Falls from our lunch, a sticky bun,
And bounces on the trampoline
Of the torn bedspread. In the mean
Distance of winter, a man sighs,
A bedstead creaks, a woman cries.

IV. JULY 14, 1951

A summer lull arrives in the West Village,
Transmuting houses into silent salvage
Of the last century, streets into wreckage
Uncalled-for by do-gooders who police
The moderniqueness of our ways, patrol
The sanitation of our urban soul.

What I mean is, devoid of people, all
Our dwellings freeze and rust in desuetude,
Fur over with untenancy, glaze grey
With summer's dust and incivility,
With lack of language and engagement, while
Their occupants sport, mutate, and transform
Themselves, play at dissembling the god Norm
From forward bases at Fire Island. But—
Exception proving rules, dissolving doubt—
Young Gordon Walker, fledgling editor,
My daylong colleague in the corridors
Of Power & Leicht, the trade-book publishers,
Is at home to the residue in his
Acute apartment in an angle of
Abingdon Square. And they're all there, the rear-
Guard of the garrison of Fort New York:
The skeleton defense of skinny girls
Who tap the typewriters of summertime;
The pale male workers who know no time off
Because too recently employed; the old
Manhattan hands, in patched and gin-stained tweeds;
The writers (Walker's one), who see in their
City as desert an oasis of
Silence and time to execute their plots
Against the state of things, but fall a prey
To day succeeding day alone, and call
A party to restore themselves to all
The inside jokes of winter, in whose caul
People click, kiss like billiard balls, and fall,
Insensible, into odd pockets. Dense
As gander-feather winter snow, intense
As inextinguishable summer sun
At five o'clock (which it now is), the noise
Of Walker's congeries of girls and boys
Foregathered in their gabbling gratitude
Strikes down the stairwell from the altitude
Of his wide-open walk-up, beckoning

Me, solo, wife gone north, to sickening
Top-story heat and talk jackhammering
Upon the anvils of all ears. "Christ, Lou, you're here,"
Whoops Walker, topping up a jelly jar
("Crabapple," says the label, still stuck on)
With gin and tonic, a blue liquid smoke
That seeks its level in my unexplored
Interior, and sends back a sonar ping
To echo in my head. Two more blue gins.
The sweat that mists my glasses interdicts
My sizing up my interlocutor,
Who is, I think, the girl who lives next door,
A long-necked, fiddleheaded, celliform
Girl cellist propped on an improbably
Slim leg. Gin pings are now continuous.
The room swings in its gimbals. In the bath
Is silence, blessed, relative, untorn
By the cool drizzle of the bathtub tap,
A clear and present invitation. Like
A climber conquering K.28,
I clamber over the white porcelain
Rock face, through whitish veils of rubberized
Shower curtain, and at length, full-dressed, recline
In the encaustic crater, where a fine
Thread of cold water irrigates my feet,
To sleep, perchance to dream of winter in
The Village, fat with its full complement
Of refugees returned to their own turf—
Unspringy as it is—in a strong surf
Of retrogressing lemmings, faces fixed
On the unlovely birthplace of their mixed
Emotions, marriages, media, and met-
Aphors. Lord God of hosts, be with them yet.

II.

A War Requiem

(To Jonathan Peale Bishop and John Cooke Dowd, Jr.)

On vit; on vit infâme. Eh bien? Il fallut l'être;
  L'infâme après tout mange et dort.
Ici même, en ses parcs, où la mort nous fait paître,
  Où la hache nous tire au sort,
Beaux poulets sont écrits; maris, amants sont dupes;
  Caquetage, intrigues de sots.
On y chante; on y joue; on y lève des jupes;
  On y fait chansons et bons mots. . . .
Et sur les gonds de fer soudain les portes crient.
  Des juges tigres nos seigneurs
Le pourvoyeur paraît. Quelle sera la proie
  Que la hache appelle aujourd'hui?
Chacun frissonne, écoute; et chacun avec joie
  Voit que ce n'est pas encore lui. . . .
                              —*André Chénier*

I. FALL PLANTING

1. New York, 1929

When Hartley Wintney went out on the town—
Immaculate conception in a brown
Twill suit from Rivers Brothers, over which
His Arrow Collar face appeared in rich
And manful tones, surmounted by his blond
Coif and a Herbert Johnson pinch-front hat—
He fared forth like a newborn bearer bond
Engrossed with promise. Think of him in that
Half-grown Manhattan, shouldering cornerstones
Aside, reflecting on old firms' brass plaques,
Damning the fluvium of limousines

In fording Madison, deflecting cabs
And westbound walkers, courting judgment from
The dumb irons of green omnibuses come
Up out of quarries of intense twilight
Between flat shafts of sun. Now picture him
Far east, as forceless early lights come on
And catch and lose the white moth of his hat.
Brownstones cringe under blue-lit windows where
Electrotypers cast out on the air
An alphabet of clatters; sewers leak
A peevish smell of garbage, a sure mark
Of early summer coming in New York.
Down brown steps he addresses a peephole,
Is recognized, and passes into Rynne's.

Four hours draw circles on the Biltmore clock.
On Forty-eighth, near Rynne's, you cannot hear
The fight inside or guess at its extent
Until a man, out cold, is dumped out in
The areaway. His hat is gone and his
Collar has been detached. One sleeve hangs off
His hundred-dollar suit. One garter shows
Up one prone leg, and claret stains his shirt.
Possessed, he rises up and walks back west
And comes upon his destination at
Almost the hour of two, according to
His father's half-case hunter watch, still in
His right-hand waistcoat pocket; comes upon
The sleeping Princeton Club, his sometime home,
And startles the night porter. "Here, you can't
Come in like that. My God, it's Mr. Wint—"
And dies there in the foyer, in the arms
Of Mr. Murtha, far from Grosse Pointe Farms.

2. New York, 1932

Shot with the huge, crude Graflexes of the period:
Sun on the stone of the baggy trouser legs
Of the men in line, on their outsize cloth caps
And hollow, woodworked faces, overexposed
To the emulsion and the elements;
Shade on the shelter, with its hasty sign,
"Soup Kitchen," in the small, prehensile loops
And stilted, stork-footed ascenders of
An old signman who learned his ornate trade
In the last flowery century; and shade
In the sharp shadows of petitioners
Longer than their slight, short significance
In history, and on the evening street
Of cast-iron mercantile establishments,
All underexposed. The line, frozen in time
And on the negative, stalls in Cooper Square.
Turn the roto page and Paul Whiteman is there.

3. Cross Corners, Mich., 1935

The bank owned half the county when it failed.
The second crop of hay, uncut, unbaled,
Stands sentry to a country town in shock.
Greenbottles buzz and bumble on the stock
In the Nyal Drug Store window, backed by pink,
Sun-faded sunbursts of crêpe paper; linked
Rings signify the vacant Odd Fellows
Hall overhead; next door, the Corner Store
Moves precious little of its short supply
Of Dubble Bubble Gum and green Nehi;
Across the street, R. Brown Purina Chows
Caters to few blue, cut-down Dodge sedans
With dangling tags; the droning standard fans
Drown out no cross talk in the Owl Café;
The sun sits regent in the boundless day.

Down by the P.M. tracks, a man in Finck's
Bib Overalls (Wears Like a Pig's Nose) thinks
Of someplace else, where, with a stunning sound
Of terrene thunder, the Express is bound.

4. *Thomas Jefferson Henderson, 1937*

At dinner in his modest palace on
Chicago Boulevard, Mr. Henderson,
The General Manager of the Frontenac
Motor Division, cuts his New York steak
Fine, finer, finest; chews mechanical
Bites into particles while listening
To Amos 'n' Andy on the glistening
Green-eyed mahogany dining-room radio,
And muses on his Southern origins,
Transcending Snopeses in the cotton gins,
And northering through his four good years at Tech
And his not happenstantial close connec-
Tions with the Chairman of the Board, Red Clay,
Whom he long served as duteous protégé,
Joker, and Georgian co-religionist,
And swarmed like lightning up the terraced list
Of top executives to Everest:
Alliance Motors' Aztec tower suite
Aloof from the contentions of the street,
Which now begins—the news comes on—to mass
Its voices and be heard through the high glass.

Drive east on Jefferson Avenue: beyond
The billboards for the All-New Fronty Eight
For '37, price $695
And up, a white four-stacker reaches up
To tie its smoke up to the smutty sky
Above the great white word, fifteen yards high,
That spells out Frontenac across the sound
Of foundry work, across the belt of smells—

Meltmetal, ozone, stove gas — that surrounds,
In clouds of visibility, the core
Of all the purposes this city's for.

Drive east and see no smoke, for once, and hear
No presses pressing on, and smell no scent
Of tractable materials being bent
To shape our ends; instead, all silence hangs
Instead of smoke up in the unmarked air;
The chain-link gates are locked, and over there
A line of lictors in blue dungarees
Bears notice of its grievance. In such peace
Lies a delusion: nightly, plant police,
Recruited on their records, deputized
For the duration, leave their paralyzed,
Emasculated, blind antagonists
For dead or worse in ditches, where the rays
Of sunrise will not interrupt their rest.

5. La Lutte Finale, 1937

Progressive Bookshop: International
Publishers' titles lap dot-eyed old men
Who scan a Spanish war map. Out of the Blue
Network, a messenger of unities,
The battle claims all ears. *Heimat ist weit:*
Mitteleuropa, clouded by the black,
Descendent shape, calls to her sons, *Freiheit!*
Meanwhile, Alpini move on Teruel,
Savoias bomb Bilbao, Falangist troops
With Schmeissers decimate the volunteers
Who post themselves — selections of the Left
Book Club — to wars they never made. A stir,
A surge to the front door: a winded old
Dispatch rider descends his bicycle
And leans, straight-armed, against the open door.
News from the front, as soon as he can speak.

"It's Jack. Jack. Jack——" A long saw-stroke of breath.
"'S dead. Jack Sharfman's dead. The telegram
Came 8 A.M. Outside Madrid. A bomb."
A son, the potency of all of them,
Lies in the bosom of the Abraham
Lincoln Battalion, mourned by all good men.

6. Rosedale Theatre, 1938

Feet on the parapet of the balcony,
We cup free sacks of penny candy, gum,
And unshelled peanuts, all included in
Our dime admission to the Saturday
Kids' matinée, and see the *Bounty* heave
And creak in every block and halyard. Waves
Of raw sensation break upon each white
Face that reflects the action, and our ears
Eavesdrop upon the commerce of a more
Real world than ours. The first big feature ends;
We trade reactions and gumballs with friends
Above the marching feet of Movietone,
Which now give way to a twin-engine plane
That lands as we half watch, and Chamberlain
Steps out, in his teeth, Homburg, and mustache,
A figure of some fun. We laugh and miss
His little speech. After the Michigan-
Ohio game, Buck Rogers will come on.

7. Athens, Ohio, 1939

"ATHENIA TORPEDOED," says today's
Press in the tourist guesthouse. "WAR IMPENDS."
Out back in the black meadow, among friends—
Some summer bugs contending, timothy's
Familiar dip and scratch behind bare knees,
The duty pool of stars—I can't believe
In such disaster being broadcast, such

Mere alien, unpermitted anarchy
Loosed on an ordered world that features me.

II. WINTERTIME AND SPRING

8. The Regiment, 1940

"The battle of liberty may one day be
Won on these playing fields of Birmingham
University School, where only last year we
Beat Grosse Pointe Country Day eighteen to three,"
Says Mr. Dunn, our stout form master, to
Our weedy rows of raw recruits — aged ten
To seventeen — in ample khaki suits.
"The regiment," he tells our understrength
Headquarters company, already whipped
By bigger winds than we are, eyes tear-gassed
By cutting gusts of late-November air,
"The regiment will serve its country well
If the day comes, and [words drowned out] the school."
The Mauser on my shoulder galls the bone.
Fat Pringle, on my left, gives a long groan.
Wan Lundy, on my right, bends in the breeze.
I snuffle and unlock my shaky knees.
"Now Captain Strong will drill the regiment
In the manual of arms before — uh — mess.
Let's show him [unintelligible phrase]
The dedication that is B.U.S."

9. Washington, 1941

The solid geometry of Washington
Goes soft and butter-edged in the solvent sun
Of May. Dark men in frogs with jingling trays
Light-foot it down the humid corridors
Of the old Willard, where the spelling-bee

Contenders—having muffed "chrysanthemum,"
"Dehiscent," "hautbois," "phthisic," lost and won
The ordeal in the auditorium—
Now wait to meet the President, each head
Stuffed with a recent residue of dead
Euclidean theorems: dome hemispheres,
Spire cones, room cubes, and pillar cylinders.
Our cicerone, a spare newspaperman,
Has news for us at breakfast: due to the
Tense impasse over lend-lease, we will not
Be introduced to Mr. Roosevelt,
Who sends sincere regrets. Instead, we will
Tour more of hot, awaking Capitol Hill,
Whose shuttered faces turn toward the pull
Of transatlantic gravity, whose will
Annihilates the longueurs of the sea.

10. Detroit, 1943

In memory of the nineteenth century,
The hobby shop I run in summertime
Observes a day of silence; opening
Up in the morning, I walk into a
Wall of still must just scented with faint thyme;
The regulator clock paces a slow
And steady measure all alone; the pressed-
Tin ceiling whimpers in the heat; and no
Small Negro boys, as beautiful as dolls,
Come for instruction in the mystery
Of modelling: a wing rib pinned down here,
Between the leading and the trailing edges, on
Wax paper, which protects the plan, and glued.
Later, the delicate stretching of the blue
Tissue over the structure, to include
It in the empyrean, and a coat
Of dark-blue dope for tautness. No black boys
Appear by noon. On my way home to lunch,

I see the smoke down Woodward Avenue
And hear a dull sea far away, where black
Is East and white is West, who fight
For lone possession of the street behind
The barricades of burning cars. My shop
Stays shut all afternoon. At dusk I hear —
Above the yawps of nighthawks diving on
Their customary roofs — the treadmill beat
Of half-tracks manned and gunned by helmèted
Troopers detailed to clear the Avenue
Of riot and its grisly residue.

11. A Day Coach, 1944

A pond of vomit in the vestibule;
Fat barracks bags to fall on in the aisle;
A scrim of smoke and sweat; shive sandwiches
In fingerprinted paper and a shrill
Orange drink, drunk lukewarm with a sodden straw;
Their hawker, barely able to support
His corporation through the teeming train;
Long sailors cocked up anyhow, asleep
In the deep waters of the empty pint
Across their knees; a soldier and a WAC
Involved in one quite indivisible
Vestment of khaki; out the window, miles.

12. The Liberal Union, 1944

Election Night. The house in Holyoke Street
Blazes with hundred-watters. Light leaks out —
Despite the brownout — to define the shape
Of things to come: a crowded, derelict,
Condemned, consensual body politic,
Gone down to ashes under the rubric
Fuel of progress; down with the republic.

Under the mansard, a long drawing room
Is stacked with shiny freshmen, one week out
From home, from under mother, and with pale
And weighty bottles of cold Pickwick Ale.
A radio reports the vote; tall Tex and Tim,
Hatching with blood-red crayons, color in
Each Democratic duchy on the map
Above the mantel, to the tramping rap
Of bottles on the floor and tenor cheers.
Off on the left, some hothead and his pal
Strike up a flaccid "Internationale."

13. *April 12, 1945*

Behind the A.M.E. Church, the first fierce
Green grass springs on the dank and disused earth
Of littered yards with mutual surprise;
The colored kid I tutor has no eyes
For algebra, but only for the boys
Who vamp a pepper game in the play yard
Outside our grated window. Steps are heard.
It's Mr. Justice, leader of the Youth
Group Program, who looks grave and calls me out
Into the vestry and tells me, in neat
Jamaican tones, "I don't know how to say
This to you, Mr. Edwards, but they say
The President is dead." "Dead?" "Yes, today.
Come with me to Mass. Avenue and have
A drink with me to him." At noon, the long
Arm of the bar is nearly empty but
For barkeep, cabbies, and the radio.
"Two Myers Rum," calls Mr. Justice, who
Explains to me, aside, "An Island drink."
The dark rum comes. With infinite courtesy,
He turns and lifts his heavy glass to me,
And says, "To the memory of your President."

14. The '46s, 1945

Alliance Motors Tower. On the ground floor
Of the postwar, six shiny Frontenacs
Rotate on turntables beneath the bright
Eyes of a bank of baby spots. Away
Back in the corners stand the surpluses,
Unlit, unsung, of the late war: a tank,
A jeep, a twenty-millimetre gun,
A cutaway of an X-24
Glycol-cooled airplane engine. On the floor
Under the lights, crowds sniff the fruits of peace:
New rubber, lacquer, leather, a perfume
Four years abeyed but unforgotten; still
A year away from the sweet people's will.

15. East Cambridge, 1949

Behind the stacked extent of Kendall Square
There is a little slum; I'll take you there,
Laden with my black brush-filled salesman's case,
Perhaps a mop or two, and, on my face,
The first sweat of the day. This is the place
We start: a neat tan toy house, gingerbread
Proud of its peaky eaves. The lady's in.
She's German, tiny, old, respectable,
Not buying anything. Next door, a tall
Blue tenement hangs open. In its hall,
The fumes of urine and the fractured wall
Don't augur well for brush men. That's all wrong.
Up the length—gaslit, railless—of the long
And aging stairwell live star customers:
Draggled and pregnant girls who fumble coins
Among contending children; pensioners,
Dressed in a skeletal state of readiness,
Who welcome all intruders bearing news
Of the last act of the world; lone, stubbled young

Men who change babies while the wife's at work.
I write the orders in my little book,
Take a deposit, promise delivery
A week from Saturday. At noon I lunch
On tonic and a Hostess Apple Pie
At Aly's Spa in Portland Street. At night,
I leave the last room with a Sacred Heart
And Kroehler furniture for my rendezvous
With Jonathan, a breath of Harvard Square
In his black '36 Ford coupe, his bare
Feet on the pedals. We abscond from there.

16. The Publisher, 1951

"Now get me Captain Alice Coddington,
The General's aide. No, she's in Washington,
For Christ's sake. O.K., try the Pentagon."
The handset hits the cradle like a gun.
Burt Seltzer lifts a large, low-calorie
Elastic band to his abnormally
Small mouth—a hotel slit for razor blades—
And chews with relish. His long fingers, which,
At first glance, seem to have an extra joint,
Play lancers with a pencil, whose sharp point
Riddles a Webster's Second Unabridged,
Open to "Minotaur." A crapulent
Bar of the best band brass bursts in the win-
Dow, and—except for Burt—we crowd around
To see the source of that preëmptive sound.
A small parade, beleaguered by a gale
Of paper snow, pursued by biped wolves
With cameras, traverses the bare, pale
Hot tundra of Fifth Avenue. Behind
The army band, a fancy phaeton
With the top down, a glittering '41
Chrysler Imperial, daunting as the sun,
Cradles the recalled General, recalled

Just as he is today, in suntan hat,
From his long and all-promising career
Halfway around our curve-ball-spinning sphere,
Halfway from earth to heaven, lit by love
Of his high mission and laid low by Jove.
"Elaine, you stupid bastard, where's my call?
Don't give me that crap. I can't wait at all.
Yeah, put me through now." Pause. A brief reprise
Of masticated rubber. "Alice? How
You doing, darling? I mean with the book?
I know it, sweetie. Sure, he just went by.
Listen—don't worry. Just remember we
Need the whole manuscript September the—
Right. O.K., honey. See you. *Ciao.* Goodbye."

III. High Summer

17. The Candidate, 1952

Archaic Boston, a splayed hand of squat
Brick business buildings laced with shire-town smells—
Roast coffee, fresh fish, lettuce, tanneries—
Cools into fall and warmly welcomes back
Its horse-faced grandees, panama'd, in black
Alpaca jackets, posting down State Street
To their renumeration on the high
Chairs of their countinghouses. Close at hand,
On Batterymarch, a plan they would deplore
Takes shape as six signmen affix a long
Hand-lettered banner to an empty store.
"O'Kane's O.K. with Massachusetts," it
Declares in characters some four feet high,
Pointedly pointed with a union bug.
Inside, I meet his campaign manager,
White-headed, red Lucretius Gallagher,
Late editor of the set Boston *Sun,*
And set to work to make a senator

At an old upright Royal in a room
Quite like a city room, and on the run
To many contacts: first, the mother of
Us all, Maureen O'Kane, the matriarch;
Next, Kath O'Kane, the sister, a thin, shrewd,
And shining foil with Niccolonian
Schemes to bring down the arch-Republican
Incumbent, Adams, on his own Palladian
Home ground; last, Kevin, the calm candidate,
Halfway between his person and the shape
Of a great figure, in the pupal stage
Of statecraft, now half-metamorphosed from
A moody, willful, and mercuric young
Man to the measured senator to come.
In his high, prosperous cell, the prisoner
Seems easy in his bonds, under the dour
And time-releasing sedative of power.

18. Brynfan Tyddyn, 1955

In the horse latitudes, there is a farm
Upon a hill in Pennsylvania.
Young men in irons pursue a mania
For motion there, surrounded by becalmed
Blood brothers in an age of stasis. Out
Of Wilkes, across the river, up the bluff
Of Forty Fort, and into the snow roll
Of ridges, we emerge upon a road
Where racing cars blur by, and consequent
Dust settles on the rye. We ease our red
A.C. down off the flatbed; John gets in
And comes back dirty from his practice laps.
The grid forms up for our heat—under two
Litres—the green flag falls, a rush-hour mass
Of cars howls off and dwindles. Silence. Smoke.
Two minutes, and a faint whine-grunt precedes
The field into the chute before the straight.

An A6 Maserati leads a light-
Blue 1.5 Osca in a scratch duet
For loud soprano six and tenor four;
John comes through third but first in class, ahead
Of sundry Bristols, and bangs on his door —
A spoof on Nuvolari — for more speed.
The standings hold for three more laps. Then John
Loses his right-rear in the pit-straight chute
And slews off down the dirt escape road, no
Power or brakes to stop him, to a stop
Deep in a stubble field, while his wild wheel
Smashes a sheriff's windshield. We retrieve
The car and load it, limp with our reprieve,
And drink our luck in tepid Stegmaier beer.

19. *Cahiers du Cinéma, 1956*

Dissolve from a proscenium arch of "L"
In Flushing to a matching arch of mike
Booms, light stands, fearless dollies, blimps inside
The building in its shade, where thirty-two
Souls stiffen at the sound of "Speed!" and clap
Of clapsticks clapping on the set. In dream,
A blond wife ambulates across a room
Built out of flats, her back lit by a Con
Edison evening sun. She's carrying
An insubstantial crown of peach ice cream
To her peach-featured, immaterial
Young holy family. She muffs a line.
Cut. Take two. Outside, by the Optimo
Cigar Store, a live, dirty, dying man
Dives for the *Daily News* in a trash can.

20. *Claremont, 1957*

It's a long, long way from the Park-Lex
Building up to that institutional

Ridge-running street between hot Harlem and
The lion Hudson. High Edwardian
Doors wrought, or wreaked, in iron let me in
To a tall, cool, dim, dull mosaic hall
Equipped with one wee elevator. On
The fifth, my friends come creeping out to greet
Me and my gift, a gift-wrapped fifth of Fitz.
Within, with Steve, the meek Chicagoan,
Escaped, by luck and struggle, from a slum,
And Ren, short for Renata, his bird-wife,
We talk a little about him: his course
In letters at Columbia, his plans —
Ten years old and still twining out in new
Directions — for his first novel, about
Writers and bookies in Chicago. And
We talk a little about me: my five-
Year plan not to write anything at all.
But mainly we discuss the threats — Bomb,
The State, Mass Media, the Thought Police —
That freeze us in our ruts and stay our hands
Upon our keys and brushes, staves and pens.

21. A Marriage, 1958

November russets flush the last of green
Out of its summer coverts; mist and frost
Condense and crystallize on lignified
Black twigs; red berries shrivel; a sad light
Undistances horizons, setting dense
Swatches of nothingness beyond the fence
In non-objective umber. We arise
At seven in our tiny country house —
The center of November, and the point
Of no return to cities, with their sour
Remarks on ruinous first marriages —
Eat eggs, dress in dark clothes, get in our black
Jaguar roadster, and in dusting snow —

The season's first, greasing the roads — we go
Across the line to Nashua, where, in
A blank room of dun office furniture,
We say our vows before a registrar
In rimless glasses, and, as witnesses,
Flower girls, trainbearers, maids of honor, two
Gum-chewing, French-accented typists, who
Congratulate us gravely when the ring
Has been slid on, when the deal-sealing kiss
Has been exchanged. Stiff handshakes all around;
A chorus of farewells; we're homeward bound
On now quite icy roads, to lunch alone
In a decrepit tearoom; to come home
To a new, mutual aloneness in
Our little house as winter enters in.

22. Writing, 1963

For years he was cross-eyed, the right eye turning in
Shyly, and he, shyly ducking his head
To hide the inturning, failed to notice the eyes
Of all the others, also in hiding from
The eyes of others, as in a painting of
The subway by Charles Harbutt. Self-denying
Can get you something if, behind the blank,
Unwindowed wall, you don't become a blank,
Unfurnished person. He was lucky. In
The dark of those bare rooms to let, there stirred
Something: a tattered arras woven with
A silent motto, as Eliot said. A word
Now, in his thirty-sixth summer, surfaces, leading
A train of thought, a manifest freight, up to
The metalled road of light — for the first time
In ten disused, interior years — along
The rusted, weed-flagged lines. And so the raid
On the inarticulate, as Eliot said,
Begins again. Square-bashing awkward squads

Of words turn right about under the sun,
Form ragged quatrains in the quiet room
Under the eaves, where his pen cuts its first
Orders in ages, and the detail moves off
The page, not quite in step, to anywhere.

23. Cambridge, 1963

A wake, without the whiskey or the words
Of eulogy, before the one blue eye
Of television in the deepening
November evening. When, earlier,
My secretary said she'd heard that he
Had just been shot, we gaped in nervous pre-
Lapsarian unbelief. Now it is not
More real but we are less so, and the scream
Calls us to places in a doomsday scene
Of national disjuncture from a show
By Wells or Welles. Lear's "never," a hoarse crow
Of omen, takes wing to the rooky wood
Of early terrors suddenly grown up,
Grown old in one weekend. A catafalque
On wagon wheels rolls, powered by muffled drums,
Down the vast desert street to which we come,
Clutching our wives and wallets, to assist
In turning nature art; in the night mist
Behind the White House, two linked silhouettes —
A great *Life* picture — cut across the lawn
To leave the sound stage and to be alone.

IV. Harvest Home

24. A Walk in Roxbury, 1964

A sense of last times. On Columbus Ave.,
A hot May day. A sky of mother-of-pearl

Brings leaves on the few trees and people on
The many front stoops out. Home-painted signs—
"The KING's," "Jack's Sharp Store," "Marnie's Bar-B-Coop,"
"Hell Fire Redeemer Church"—illuminate
Exhausted brownstone streets, the hand-me-downs
Of cold-roast Boston in Victorian
Days of white hope and glory, whose new voice,
Litigious, rich, impoverished, mocking, coarse,
And fine, hangs heavily on the alien air
Above the grunt of traffic, rising where
A printed sign points out the Peppermint
Lounge Sip-In. I adjust my Nikons and
Begin to photograph a happy crowd
Preparing for an outing. They do not
Protest or even notice me, though they
And I both know that this year is the last
Of truce and toleration, and the line
Between us broadens as I zoom the lens
Back to wide-angle. I still have the print
Here. How far off those smiling holiday
Faces and their stopped laughter are today.

25. Talking Union, 1964

The liberator of the laboring
Classes is interviewed on "Meet the Press."
The ruffian who led the Frontenac
Sit-down is missing; his aged surrogate
Is a stout statesman, silver-polled and -tongued,
And silver-tied over a white-on-white
Dress shirt under a trig, if Portly, suit
Tailored by Weatherill. His priestly, bluff
Face with its large pores dryly swallows up
All pointed questions; his brown coin-purse mouth
Doles out small change wrapped in the florid scrip
Of Federalese: "parameters," "key gains,"
"Judgmentally," "negated," "targeting,"

"So, gentlemen, you see." So gentlemen
Are made, not born, with infinite labor pains.

26. Rockville, Illinois, 1965

Above the corn, the vanes of Rockville gleam,
Aloof, an island in the severed stream
Of Illinois, which feeds a landlocked lake
And never goes to sea. Here in the heart-
Land, I am right where I came in: the in-
Termitting thirty years of prosperous
Accretions have glossed over the plat, plain
Life of the plain people; have made them rich
In dollars, acres, air conditioning
Against the prairie heat, but largely not
In spirit. Still, their hospitality
Comes easy, and the chairman of the board
Of the Rockville National is open as
The barefoot farm boy with a string of mud
Cat he once was, or, rather, thinks that he
Once was and permanently ought to be.
But touch a nerve of doubt, and property
Is ringed with tense defenders: hollow squares
Of fattening Minute Men leap from their shares
To raise their automatic arms against
The roll of interlopers, black and red,
The union agitators and the fed-
Eral animal, sow and juggernaut,
That suckles at their wallets and will squat
On their rights soon. Tornado clouds of fear
Raise sickles over Rockville, tier on tier.

27. An Estrangement, 1966

Webb Beatty, having drunk too much at lunch
In some dark dive where food is only served
To justify attendance, tells me his

Troubles: how Penny, his long-standing wife
Is nipping sherry all day long and rye
All evening; how the hard goods of her ends—
"A Kelvinator, Christ's sake, with a dec-
Orated door, and that old Cadillac"—
Foul up his airy, ivory ideal
Of how to live, and blight his middle age
With bills and sorrows; how Lucinda Fry,
A junior buyer with a jocund eye
And small but gold-filled charms, has solaced him
In the broad daylight of her little room
At lunchtime, making him a feast of sheets
And steam fresh from her shower; how he may throw
His dead-end life up, and may even go
Away alone to a far shore to start
A new one, packing only shirts and heart
In his light luggage; how, in that sunset,
He and Lucinda will find all content,
And paint and write in concert as Bach plays
Behind them all their minuends of days.
His words slur now; his face slips out of shape
And into neutral; white wings of escape
Beat at his ears. He reaches for the check
And misses it. I pick it up and tell
Him nothing but the truth: I wish him well.

28. *New York, 1967*

Eyes flick blades out from under low lids, and
Turn down again to fasten on the sparks
Struck by the sidewalk. My eyes meet that tide
Halfway: the same aloofness, the same stab
Of quick cognition, the same lowering
Of sights to shoe lane, having sized them up
And put them down for good. The girls require
A little longer for each dancing breast
And mincing leg. Only the mannequins

In Bonwit's windows render me a straight,
Blank stare, which I return in kind. The Pan
Am Building, in its jointed corridors,
Affords relief: acquaintances are cut
Off neatly by their bends, and nearer friends
Truncated, disembodied, guillotined
By abstract passages and unseen doors
In a new social contract of surreal
Withdrawal and avoidance, an absurd
Theatre without end and without word.

29. *Two Candidates, 1968*

A private conversation in a room
Rife with the public and the press. Amid
White sheets of flashlight, the hot, desperate
Advance men poised to seize the candidate
And whisk him to his next engagement, late
As ever, he lets fall a casual
Comment upon the state of poetry;
Laughs lightly over an egregious lie
Expounded by an arch-opponent; cites
The over-erudite allusions of
Another rival to the ancient Greek.
"That's Aeschylation in political
Quotation," he remarks in a slow, calm
Voice at the middle of the maelstrom.
The other office seeker occupies
A lidded bed under the gritty eyes
Of gleaming notabilities, a guard
Of honor changed at each night hour; the eyes
Of those unknowns who, in a double line,
Reach backward out the great church doors, around
The block behind the buttresses; the eyes
Of early watchers high up in the sun-
Struck monolith across the street, who see,
At length, a coffin carried out; the eyes

Of mourners at the stops along a route
Just the reverse of Lincoln's; the dry eyes
Of the most high and lowly in the long,
Decayed, redounding concourse of the Un-
Ion Station; late, the eyes of Washington.

30. *New York, 1968*

The surf of traffic in the arteries
Of evening inundates all ears; in crosstown streets,
It is occluded by occasional
Yells, ash cans falling, Sanitation trucks
Regurgitating garbage, witching cries,
A crystalline lone footstep with a limp,
And Robinson's phone ringing in his flat.
Still, sometimes our small noise and voice are heard
Above the melancholy, long, advancing roar
Of transit reaching up the beach of our
Old ananthropocentric island, to
The bass of the night wind, and we come true
To one another, till the rising town's
Unhuman voices wake us, and we drown.

31. *Thirty Thousand Gone, 1968*

In CONUS, whence all blessings flow, I drive
To Ayer for beer. On our road, amber flares
Ripen like grapefruit in a grove of air
Fast growing dark. Down in the valley, small-
Calibre guns begin long, gibbering
Dialogues out beyond the mock Perfume
River, really the smelly Nashua.
Tank engines ululate. In Vietnam
Village, street fighters infiltrate the set
Of simulated buildings, while fléchette
Canisters fired by 105's protect
The point with sheets of tissue-shredding darts.

The heavies enter. Flashes shatter night
And impacts puncture my unruffled drum-
Roll of exhaust. In Ayer, the archetype
Of post towns, with its scruffy yellow-brick
Two-story business blocks, shut shops, bright bars,
It's pay night. In the orchid neon light
Shed by the Little Klub, a herd of ponycars
Grazes an asphalt pasture. Feat M.P.'s
Snuff out a flash fight at the Hotel Linc.
A Charge burns a little rubber to
Arrest two ready, wary, cruising girls
Whose buttocks counter-rotate down Main Street.
'Nam veterans in troop boots and a chest
Awash with medal ribbons stare down knots
Of new recruits, high on Colt 45.
The Package Store is all decorum. Men
In black bow ties wait coolly on the boys,
Their guns and clubs prudentially concealed
Behind the counter. With my six-pack, I
Leave town, passing an Army ambulance
With beacon on and siren winnowing
The road ahead. A yellow GTO
Has flipped atop the railroad bridge, and bare-
Armed viewers with mauve cheeks, purpureal
Eyes, lavender-green lips in mercury-
Vapor-lamp light look on in ecstasy
At others' errors. From the overpass
On the road back, I see a divisional
Convoy bound westward, double strands of lights
Strung clear back to the third ridge, coming on
Slowly, preserving prescribed intervals,
Diminishing the other way in one
Long red ellipsis, going, going, gone
Into the red crack that still separates
The blue-black air from blue-black earth: the gates
At the world's end. The battle on our hill
Still rants and tatters nighttime till a red

Flare, like a larger Mars, can supervene
And make a false arrest of everything.
The last burst dies; the battlefield goes dark;
Cicadas sizzle; towns away, dogs bark.

V. In the New Year

32. Twelfth Night, 1969

Snowbound on Twelfth Night, in the interact
Of winter, in the white from green to green,
I warm myself in isolation. In
The aura of the fire of applewood
With its faint scent of McIntoshes, in
The disappearing act of the low sun,
A marginally yellow medallion
Behind the white snow sky, under the in-
Undation of sharp snowdrifts like the fins
Of sharks astride our windowsills, I hide
Out in my hideout from the memory
Of our unlovely recent history,
And of those fresh divisions just gone west.
A sharp sound brings me back: perhaps a tree
Cleft by the cold, but likelier the crack
Of a gun down at Devens. Snow begins
To lance against the window, and I see,
By luck, a leisurely and murderous
Shadow detach itself with a marine
Grace from an apple tree. A snowy owl,
Cinereous, nearly invisible,
Planes down its glide path to surprise a vole.

from

Pursuit of Honor

The Big Rock-Candy Mountain

(To the memory of my half brother, Winfield Shannon,
itinerant farm worker, 1909–1969)

A mason times his mallet
to a lark's twitter . . .
till the stone spells a name
naming none,
a man abolished.
              —*Basil Bunting*

I. "ON A SUMMER'S DAY IN THE MONTH OF MAY,
    A JOCKER COME A-HIKING
    DOWN A SHADY LANE IN THE SUGAR CANE,
    A-LOOKING FOR HIS LIKING. . . ."

The land was theirs after we were the land's,
The visionaries with prehensile hands—
The Wobblies, Okies, wetbacks—driven and drawn
To cross the land and see it, to select
A tree to lie out under: a Pound Sweet,
A Cox's Orange Pippin, a pecan,
Persimmon, Bartlett, quince, Bing, freestone, fig,
Grapefruit, Valencia. The trundling trains
That took their supercargo free are gone,
And so are they; a thousand circling camps
Down by the freight yards are dispersed, watchfires
Burnt out, inhabitants transshipped
To death or terminal respectability
In cold wards of the state, where their last rites
Are levied on the people, ritual
Gravediggers of the past, ratepayers for

A lot in potter's field. Old Gravensteins,
Bedight with morbid branches, shelter no
Transients at length. Our suburbs saw them go.

II. "AS HE ROAMED ALONG, HE SANG A SONG
OF THE LAND OF MILK AND HONEY,
WHERE A BUM CAN STAY FOR MANY A DAY
AND HE WON'T NEED ANY MONEY. . . ."

Uninterest in progress was their crime,
Short-circuited ambition. They came out
On a Traverse County hilltop one late-May
Morning and gave an involuntary shout
At those square miles of cherry blossom on
The slopes above the lake; exclaimed at wheat,
Fat in the ear and staggered in the wind,
In Hillsdale County; up in Washtenaw,
Spoke to the plough mules and the meadowlark
A little after dawn; in Lenawee,
Laughed at a foal's first grounding in the art
Of standing in the grass. Too tentative,
Too deferent to put down roots beside
Us in our towns, outcast, outcaste, they rode
Out of our sight into the sheltering storm
Of their irrelevant reality:
Those leagues of fields out there beyond the pale
Fretting of cities, where, in prison clothes,
We cultivate our gardens for the rose
Of self redoubled, for the florid green
Of money succulent as cabbage leaves.
They have gone out to pasture. No one grieves.

III. "OH, THE BUZZING OF THE BEES IN THE CIGARETTE TREES,
THE SODA-WATER FOUNTAIN,
THE LEMONADE SPRINGS WHERE THE BLUEBIRD SINGS
ON THE BIG ROCK-CANDY MOUNTAIN. . . ."

A young man on a Harley-Davidson
(An old one painted olive drab, with long-
Horn handlebars and a slab-sided tank),
You pushed your blond hair back one-handed when
You stopped and lit a Camel cigarette.
You laughed and showed white teeth; you had a blond
Mustache; wore cardigans and knickerbockers; wowed
The farm-town girls; drank beer; drew gracefully;
Fell, frothing at the mouth, in a grand mal
Seizure from time to time. In your small room
In Grandpa's house, you kept your goods: pastels,
A sketching block, a superheterodyne
Kit radio, a tin can full of parts,
A stack of *Popular Mechanics,* three
Kaywoodie pipes, an old Antonio
Y Cleopatra box for letters and
Receipts, a Rexall calendar with fat
Full moons controlling 1933.

IV. "OH, THE FARMER AND HIS SON, THEY WERE ON THE RUN,
   TO THE HAYFIELD THEY WERE BOUNDING.
   SAID THE BUM TO THE SON, 'WHY DON'T YOU COME
   TO THAT BIG ROCK-CANDY MOUNTAIN?' . . ."

When Grandpa died and your employer died,
And the widow sold off his tax-loss horse farm
(Those Morgans being auctioned, going meek
To new grooms less deft-handed than you were,
To new frame stables and new riding rings),
You hit the road at fifty and alone
Struck out cross country lamely, too damned old
To keep up with the kids or keep out cold
Except with whiskey, cheap and strong. Too long
You hiked from job to picking job, and when
Snow plastered stubble laths, you holed up in
The Mapes Hotel for winter; did odd jobs
To keep in nips of Richmond Rye; dozed through

The night till spring; fared forward once again
To summer's manufactory, a mill
Of insect tickings on a field of gold,
And fall's great remnant store. Last winter, you
Spent your last winter in a coffining
Dead room on Third Street in Ann Arbor, where
Only the landlady climbed up your stair
And passed your unknocked door in sateen mules.

V. "SO THE VERY NEXT DAY THEY HIKED AWAY;
    THE MILEPOSTS THEY KEPT COUNTING,
    BUT THEY NEVER ARRIVED AT THE LEMONADE TIDE
    ON THE BIG ROCK-CANDY MOUNTAIN. . . ."

In Goebel's Funeral Home, where row on row
Of coffins lie at anchor, burning dark
Hulls—walnut, rosewood—on a light-blue tide
Of broadloom, we select Economy—
Grey fibreglass with a white-rayon shroud
And mainsheets—and stand out into the street,
Becalmed already in the April heat
That conjures greenness out of earthen fields,
Tips black twigs pink on trees, starts habit's sweat
Out of Midwestern brows. In Winfield's room,
A cave of unstirred air kept in the dark
By pinholed shades, we shift his transient
Things in a foredoomed hunt for permanent
Memorials. No photograph, no ring,
No watch, no diary, no effects. Nothing—
Beyond a mildewed pile of mackinaws
(On top) and boots (precipitated out)—
Except the lone cigar box. On its lid
A rampant Antony advances on
Bare-breasted Cleopatra, areoles
Red as lit panatelas, but inside,
Only a heap of fingered rent receipts,
On pale-green check stock, weights a linen pad

Of Woolworth letter paper. Here begins
Winfield's last letter, in a corn-grain-round,
School-Palmer-Method hand riven by age,
Drink, sickness: "April 17. Dear Folks—
The weather has warmed up some but I don't"
No more. The hospital bed intervened.
Peritonitis. Coma. Peaceful death.
In truth it is. In Goebel's viewing room
The guest has been laid out, now neat, now dressed—
In shirt, tie, jacket—as if for a feast.
It is not over-stressed. He looks his age
(Not brotherly at all; avuncular,
Judicious, a thought sallow, robbed of the
Brilliance of his two straight and sky-blue eyes)
And takes his silent part upon the stage
Miming repose, an unemotional
Exit dictated by the prompter's page.
Later, in the three-car processional
To the old graveyard, we ride just behind
His Stygian Superior hearse, a Cadillac.
The grave has been dug under tamaracks;
The young Episcopalian minister
Dispassionately, as he should for one unknown
To him, says the set words designed to send
The dead off; soon the open grave will close,
The mason test his chisel and begin,
Tabula rasa, to cut that name in-
To his blank slab of granite, much as that
Void grave will take the imprint of his weight,
And all his travels will be at an end.

ENVOY

But, prince that fortune turned into a toad,
Instead I see you—camped beside a road
Between old fruit trees in full bloom in May—
Lie out under an agèd Pound Sweet and

Sleep soundly on the last night of your way
Out of a rifled and abandoned land.

Lieder Eines Fahrenden Gesellen:
A Mouth-Organ Tune

Jesus, is Schimmer a flaky son of a bitch.
Listen what happened Friday. This is rich.
Friday he threw a party in his pent-
House. East End Avenue. Invitations went
Out one month early. All embossed, addressed
By secretaries, with—get this—a crest—
His monogram, for Christ's sake—on the flap.
Maida and I, we put on all this crap—
A costume party, *you* know. I was Gen-
Ghis Khan, she was the fair Maid Marian
In a green doublet slashed right down the front.
You should of seen it. Anyway, we went.
Got there right on the tick. Big hullaballoo
Already under way. Celebs. Champagne.
An eight-piece folk-rock combo. At least two
Bars in each room, pouring booze like rain.
And right in the sunken conversation pit
In the living room, there was this thing, floodlit
From up above: a funk-art statue of
A cop in a crash hat, standing above
A dead kid tangled in his motorbike,
All one side blood. I never seen the like,
It was so real. So still. It shook us up.
But we got over it and had a cup
Of Schimmer's punch and looked at his Jim Dines.
All of a sudden hell broke loose. At nine,
The dead-kid statue suddenly stood up,
Climbed on his bike and started it. The cop

Whipped out his gun and fired it as the kid
Took off out through the foyer. Panic! Did
That party ever come to a sudden stop!
Of course, it was a put-on. Schimmer hired
A couple actors. The bullets the cop fired
Were blanks. The blood was phony, too. What some
Wise bastards won't do just to have some fun.

In Bardbury

(For John Malcolm Brinnin)

"This ere is what," says Mr. Carpenter,
The coffin foreman, in a herringbone
Waistcoat and gold-rimmed spectacles obtained
On the National Health, no doubt, "This ere is what—"
And points one digit to a neatly joined
And midget casket, just, to judge from the
Miasma of acetone, neatly cellulosed
In a suitable baby white, "This ere is what
We buried the remains of Mr. Eliot
In out there," pointing to the churchyard of
St. Muse. "And shockin little of im there was:
Two little volumes not ardly bigger than the
Basingstoke telephone book." With which he shook
His ploughshare nose and a colorless drop fell off.
"Now look at this ere": a rod-long oak box,
Full fathom wide, wood dark as blackbeetles.
"This ere size is the one we ad to use
To plant the Poet Laureate, if you'll excuse
My French. More books than a ole libary."
Thanks, Mr. Carpenter, for the florin tour
Of Plume & Sons' back room. I point my broad-
Stub nose toward the moist, unpainted air
And pad out past the bone booths in their rows

To the green-grown, grey-pocked graveyard right out there,
Patrolled by stick-straight Mr. Sacrister
In his green-grown grey cerement.
"Two new memorials of special note
You'll wish to look at, sir," he says, by rote,
And courteously conducts my crofted arm
To one small marble marker, two by two,
Charged with her arms and "By Appointment to
H. M. the Queen her Poet Laureate."
The tumulus extends five yards in front of it.
A pause. Mist drips from lindens. My guide clears
His throat, discreet. "On this side, sir, we ave
The other monument." A minute's walk.
Above the tiny mound, a tall Trajan's
Column materializes out of moist
And pearl-grey air. A cool Ionic plinth
Incised with one chaste E. A fluted shaft
As great in girth as any tree, which shades
Up into thickening mist and disappears.
"Massive but tasteful, sir, I'd say." The yews
Drizzle in silence on St. Muse.

A Loss of Largess; Its Recapture
(And Point After)

(For John Updike)

Where are the belles of yestere'en, where Harkness
Reared Gothathletic pinnacles on darkness,
Where sate their dim dams in effasive, noctious
Harmonic bombazines, at least an octave
Over the battle? Where are those dames, dangled
On stringlings above mantels lit with bangled
Epergnes and lustres, ordering with mingled
Parade-ground basses and restraint-enstrangled

Triangle tingles of politesse their embalmy
Crack cakewalk waxwork corps d'élite of calmly
Extinguishing retainers going dark?
Today we have the proceeds in the park
Of their harbinging; in the standard carks
Conveyed by every face in every car
That laterals across from bar to bar,
Completed in the end zone of the high
Sixties; in the infirm plasticity
Of talltale fictions in the plastic city
Sent up, shot down (short life, short art) by those
Gallinulistic whooping cranes that raze
All parallelepipeds here below in G's
Good time, the sucaryllic by and by;
In how sad steps the dancers from the dance
At yon new discothèque take home, their pens-
Eroso tragic masks replaced to fie
Upon the desert teatray of the sky
And the uneasy vacuum of the street
Diminuendo to a dusty point
Of vanishing; in preternatural taints
Of outlandish unlikeness on each lass-
Itudinous pale pancake female face
Sub specie aeternitatis, less
Real than ideal in the race
For surety and demonstrata, damned
To disaffection and unravelling
In our unspacious, curt time-travelling.
Las! Las! Those belles wring out our witchèd larmes
Of lamentation for passé, accomp-
Li, done and done in in the niche of pomp
In progress ruckwards in the new-moon stone
Of night. Lick, lick, light, at the eastern hem
Of rich ink arrases, whose only son
Is born anew and dries our eyes with his
Frank, pink, unfaceable first sight; his light
Breeze dawns on us and islands us in calm,

Slow-moated selffulness. A fiddler crab
Crawls cancrizantally across the slab
Of pine to pencils, handsels one upright,
And imperceptively begins to write
On the blued goldfields of a legal pad—
Past Karnak, Babylon, Larissa, Rome,
Londinium, Firenze, Washington,
And the last sad daguerreotype of home
That the late holocaust consumed and curled—
The next line in the last act of the world.

J.J.'s Levée, 1946

Awaking way up in the eaves of Lowell House,
Facing the East, where trouble always starts,
Opening his one blue eye to meet the sun's
One red one, J.J. crooks his back and farts.

His hand feels for the glass on the nightstand,
Ticking the empty glass of muscatel,
Finally finding the one with the blue glass
Eye rolling gently in the tiny swell.

Into its squirming socket with a suck
Just like a kiss his bogus eyeball goes;
Up he now sits and strips his T-shirt off
And picks black putty from between his toes.

Weighing one hundred ten pounds soaking wet
And standing five feet, seven inches tall,
With a pigeonhole in his chest big as your fist,
J.J. sings in his shower, "Bless 'em all."

He maps a life: first east from Central Square
(His point of origin), bachelor of arts

And master too, wit, rake, and bon viveur
And gift to every girl of foreign parts.

Then to get grey and great at the big feet
Of pundits, learning hard new A, B, C
(The secret one that spells out man his fate),
In kindergarten to the Nth degree.

Now in his forty-dollar flannel suit
One size too big, and his one-dollar tie
One inch too wide, J.J. picks up his books
And goes right out to live and later die.

J.J.'s ENVOY

"All bleeding men and women ought to get
A bloody great gold medal for their pain
And duty in the face of certain death:
The Order of the W.C. with Chain."

from

Hello, Darkness

I.

Love Day, 1945*

> Slowly the ancient seas,
> Those black, predestined waters rise
> Lisping and calm before my eyes,
> And Massachusetts rises out of foam
> A state of mind in which by twos
> All beasts browse among barns and apple trees
> As in their earliest peace, and the dove comes home.
>
> — *Anthony Hecht*

I. MINUS ONE

1. Averil Sayward Snow

Imprimis, in her shower in Quincy Street,
The lady vanishes and reappears,
Venusian, in an ocean spume of steam,
And stands, material, on her bathmat—
Pink, white, and twenty-three—and dries her feet.
Naked, she to her naked face applies
A thin clay skin, and to her bare green eyes
Brown underlines, which will italicize
Her ultimate impression. A mute rose

---

* L-Day—or Love Day, in Navy parlance—was the official
designation for the date of the Okinawa landings, April 1, 1945.

Buds on her noiseless lips, and an Arpège
Of scent spans all her octaves. Into clothes
She skin-dives skillfully, emerging whole
And foliate in a war-torn world whose leaves
Too often stem from embarkation, as
Did Charley Snow's. (Please figure to yourself
Particulars of severance in the rain
In terminal night light beside the green
Sleeper, Shoshone Falls. Enough.) Now grass,
Now flesh widow, combatant unaware
In unknown actions, Averil descends
Her meat-and-mothball-smelling stairs, which end
In many mailboxes. The glass door gives
On a dank night of Germinal, the last of March.

2. Marshall Schoen

Schoen, pale and flued in black, girt in a white
Bath towel, sacks his tottering chest of drawers
In search of underwear. Big books fall down:
Thick Skeat and Onions, gamy Partridge, firm
And appetizing Whiting, solid Flesch.
Once natatorially attired, he now
Dons don's apparel: a black flannel suit
From Hunter Haig, pink shirt, illicit knit
Tie bearing Pudding colors, grape-juice shoes,
And is the utter lecturer, complete
As any man can be at twenty-two.
He smokes a Raleigh standing and rereads
A hortatory letter full of grief,
Foreknowledge, and commercial wisdom, in
An old man's unskilled hand, on his old man's
Dry-cleaning letterhead from Bedford Ave.
("Spotting Our Specialty"). Immaculate,
He slams the tin door to his tutor's suite —
Lowell G-46 — and drums his steel
Taps down the steps toward the trashy scent

Of ice-out in the river, borne by drops
Of mist that frost his horny spectacles.

3. Charley Snow

Somewhere off Okinawa, a DD
Makes for her station as a picket in
The outer radar screen. The tumulous seas
Break over her forepeak as her exec.,
Lieutenant Snow, relinquishes the conn
And goes below to take a trick of sleep
In his scant cabin, peopled by a framed
Portrait by Bachrach of his Averil
In sweet-girl-graduate cashmere and pearls.
He sleeps; the *John E. Hagan* alternates
Between beam-ends; the wardroom fiddles field
The anchor-marked but errant coffee cups;
The radar's catcher's mitt revolves above.
Thus ends his Minus One, thus enters Love
Day, April Fool's, and covers Charley Snow
With darkness till the winds of morning blow
Like sirens in the rigging, and the blips
Begin to cluster on the scanner's map.

II. L-DAY

1. Marshall

Schoen, waking, files a variance of light,
And knows he is not home; recalls last night,
Embodied still in Averil at his side;
Hears hunts of bells in ancient order ride
Out to enounce an Easter rising of
A sun, a Son, a nation twenty-nine
Years earlier, and, from his lover's bed,
A newborn Schoen, who, shaken, sees the pearl

Of morning fall like hail upon his arm,
Upon the peeling windowsill, upon
The Ford-strewn street outside, upon the Yard
Diminishing away in its chaste pale
Beneath the magic realism of
Its elms and bells, upon — turn back — the arm
Of Averil outside the covers. Schoen,
Like to his western homophone, completes
His manifest destiny: to penetrate
The world and person of the earlier
Arrivistes, keepers of the general store
Of fashions, notions, drygoods, who decline —
Agèd and inbred — to elect a fine
Young newcome to entrap their daughter's hand,
Their bolts and boxes, language, life, and land.

2. Averil

Revert to Averil, on whose eyelids light
White arts of morning, on whose ears repeal
The bells, rescinding silence. Through a slim
Slit fringed with lashes, she first apprehends
The sheet her blond arm pinions to her side;
Next, the next pillow, wrinkled, vacant, void
Of its oppressor; next, the high-hung room
Alive with light in a particulate
Manner, like mica; next, cut out of black,
But deckled white on every edge, his back
Framed in the window, a flat souvenir
Of the dimensionality of night
That had at her repose, a sharp unlike
Those cutouts of her ancestors — enshrined
In cover glasses — retrogressing up
The stairs of her house in West Cedar Street.
No, this is a new silhouette for her;
A step beyond her east to a frontier
Where new men cross the customs barrier,

Home in on her flat-lit retreat, and fill
Her bed with new, kinetic night. She smiles —
Just testing, just conducting maiden trials
Of her first real commission, of her first
Deep-water venture out of the milk-white,
Cream-calm home harbor — shivers, and, awake,
Shams sleep and prays the Lord her soul to take.

III. Plus Five

1. Charley

Dead in the water, her main battery
Out of commission, fire in the engine room
Making a black smoke marker two miles high,
The *Hagan* lists and settles for a lull
Between attacks. The slap of seas, the cries
Of wounded in the wardroom are subdued
Again by planes and guns (the forties sound
Like fists upon tin tables; twenties purr
Like muffled air compressors). Now Group One
Abandons ship; a hundred treading men
Watch in the water as a Zero weaves
Inside the guard of forties — a pale cowl
Blackened with oil and exhaust, two red
Roundels beneath the wingtips — and explodes
Amidships as his wingman, well alight,
Straddles the foredeck and goes up. Fire flows;
The ready-ammunition drums go off;
The weather, making up, sends a great swell
Under the ship and breaks her back. She sinks.
Men swim in the first silence in a week.
Two hours pass and an SC comes to glean
Survivors from the waters. Nearly two
Hundred are rescued, not including Snow.

2. Averil

Averil, at this selfsame moment, bends
Her dawning eyes upon a book of dawn's
Language, at least in English: an old green-
Bound Anglo-Saxon reader. Kennings swim
Before her in the whale road, and she kens
The sense of continuity: the men
Upon her husband's ship upon the sea;
The women here at home in the mead hall;
Their comforters upon that bed, asleep
After love's labors, lost to the wide world
Of search and service Charley Snows are born,
Not made, to man; the waiting game of her
Kind, womankind, Penelopes who must
Not fend off suitors in the interim
Nor stand on principle, on pain of dust.
What love she bears for that poor man who sleeps
Within her benison, beneath the deeps
Of purpose realized, desire fulfilled;
She covers him against the coming cold.

IV. PLUS THIRTY-SEVEN

1. Marshall

Of that long, soft, and early-bearing spring
The warmest day to date comes, carrying
The rumor of the bells, too many and strong
To let the rumors of newsboys along
Mount Auburn Street be heard. The Lowell bells—
Unmatched and matchless—now take up the call
With jingling thunder in an imbecile
Outburst of joy. Outside, the sparrows in
The Fly Club hedge sing, audibly, "V-E!"
And many a passenger wears an unwilled grin
To think that that's all over. Marshall Schoen

Marches, on a more sombre errand, north,
In his most sable suit and most subdued
Knit tie, a mourning brassard almost on
The dark stuff of his sleeve. Northward to grieve—
And not as any member of the wake,
But as a rank outsider on the black
Edge of disaster's cloud of celebrants—
He goes, untempted by the blossoming
Delicatessen of a Cambridge spring,
Unleviated by the lifting of
A six-year siege, unmoved by his late love.
When he arrives at Christ Church, that slight frame
Survival of an age of easy grace
Complete with shrine—a Tory bullet hole
Preserved in the pine reliquary of
Its thin grey sides—he sees a black pigtail
Of straggling mourners disappearing in
To hear Lieutenant Snow absolved of sin
Posthumously, and coolly eulogized
In the embalming tones of Dr. Wise,
The well-loved Rector. Standing on the brick
Sidewalk outside, arms folded, chin down, Schoen
Shakes his head once and marches home again.

2. Averil

World's youngest widow, in R. H. Stearns weeds—
Black veil, for once across an unmarked eye,
Black tailleur on a proper figure, black
Pumps cantilevering a perfect calf—
Twines black-gloved hands as if, though not, in prayer,
Drops chin, blinks back no shadow of a tear,
Shakes her head shortly once, as if to clear
Inconsolation out of it, and dumb
To Dr. Wise's plashing words, and numb
To that small throng of ill- and well-wishers
Who drill her back with ravening, unveiled
Eyes bright with speculation, sits her mount—

An off-white pew — with ladylikeness, which
Is one thing she knows cold, and perseveres.
What they don't know, although they know a lot,
Is at the moment still her secret: what
The numerous troop of non-red-letter days
Investing her desk calendar now says,
Predictably, is sure to come. A crux
Of time forms in her mind; Love Day recedes,
All its cross-purposes self-cancelling;
Today a war and man of war both come
To their dead end; tomorrow, unremarked
For anything, will be a day at home
For Averil, beside herself with due
Bills to be honored; for the first time, too,
Possessed, perhaps, of the resources she
Will need to meet them. A recessional
Hymn strikes up in Christ Church, Episcopal.

At the Bar, 1948

McBride's. Round tables in a cellar off the Square
Give point to your intensive, angular
Embodiment. In this sub-basement of
The Tower of Babel, full of talk of love
Which glances off our faces, we conclude
Our business over stingers, each betrayed
By an embezzling partner. In whose bed
Did we commit each other's substance to
A voided contract, countersigned with no
Co-maker's name? No matter. In this place
Of love and excrement, only the face
Of one's true love is legal tender. All
The tubes and armatures behind the wall
Of superfice, red conduits and blue
Recirculation systems, all the two-
Way valves are immaterial to this

Low-lighted limbo where the random wish
Is father to the title deed of love.
Now that the glittering Indian gift we gave
Returns on ruffled waters, and we drown
Unbuoyant sorrows and ourselves go down
Below the surface of a sea of young,
Or, rather, one-year-younger lovers, long
Sea-miles behind us, and the jukebox plays
Our old song, "Kiss me once and kiss me twice,"
We leave these latitudes for the blank beach
Of singleness, beyond the utter reach
Of those warm waters. In the Brattle Cab
I realize you're drunk. Arrived, you stab
Your front door with a key and stumble in.
I help you up the steps, a stranger in
Your house and person. At the top you turn
To bar the way to me. Your kiss will burn —
Hard, acid, alcoholic — on my face
For many a measured mile, a stinging trace
Of our unfounded and spontaneous
Combustion in the desert of our dust.

A Late Good Night

(For Julian Moynahan)

I. SHOP TALK

Sven Nilsson was a wizard motor mechanic.
See here: him posed, a king, in the swelling bosom
Of his poor family: fat wife, thin kids,
A suckling babe, a night-black Labrador,
A tacky cottage on the bulldozed fringe
Of an unseemly suburb. When his hands,
Passed tools by all of us in surgical
And silent pantomime, undid head studs,

Chipped, milled, and chamfered surfaces, torqued nuts
Down to the last inch-pound, slid pistons in-
To clean new bores, pressed interference fits
With strength and tact in equal measure, he
Reigned effortlessly in his mystery.

II. AFTER HOURS

When he, however, knocked off work, the black
Boyg of dark Nordics walked him down the street
To Harley's Bar, where boilermakers made
His darkness manifest. Humped on a stool,
He'd drink for hours in silence, hating what
He'd come to: a fine mind, fit for abstruse
Transactions, but unschooled and chained to a
Long, facile, crack-nailed pair of hands inlaid
With years of grease and carbon. His Munch face,
A black-fringed white wedge riven from the moon,
Would fall and fall like a storm glass until
It waned to nothing in the shadow, and he'd wake
To hump himself unsteadily back home.
Late summer, seaboard-humid: one dog night,
He took a shortcut home along the tracks,
And fell asleep beside them, where a train,
Shunting and snuffling late toward the yards,
Fell on him undefended and cut off
His good right hand. A milkman found him there,
All bloody in the muggy milk of dawn,
And drove him, severed hand and all, to the
Town hospital, where they sluiced pints of blood
Back into him and sewed his hand back on.

III. AFTERWARD

It took, and so did life. Sven, in a sweet
Trance brought on by a taste of borrowed time,
Allowed the young Dunne brothers, his patrons

And friends, to form a cordon sanitaire
Of love about him, and to isolate
Him from his hunter, nothingness, in a
Long rataplan of small talk about cars
And books and politics. But how can you,
As Julian Moynahan says, convey your love
To one convinced of his own worthlessness?
One winter's night, just having buttoned up
His last MG-TF, and having sat
Alone at Harley's Bar until last call,
Sven headed home again along the tracks,
The new snow creaking underfoot, and slowed,
And stopped, and fell asleep, curled on the rail.
A train cut him in two. He marked his last
Position with iced blood upon the snow.

IV. Now

Could anyone have done what we could not?
I doubt it very much. Some stars are born
Out of our context, and proceed alone
Upon their rounds to some far rendezvous
Dictated by their hue and magnitude,
And, to our joy and terror, flare and die.

Cockaigne: A Dream

CHORUS OF ALL: Then our Age was in it's Prime,
Free from Rage, and free from Crime,
A very Merry, Dancing, Drinking,
Laughing, Quaffing, and unthinking Time.
    (Dance of Diana's Attendants. Enter Mars.)
         —*"The Secular Masque," by John Dryden*

Coming around the corner of the dream
City I've lived in nights since I was ten—

Amalgamated of a lost New York,
A dead Detroit, a trussed and mummified
Skylineless Boston with a hint thrown in
Of Philadelphia and London in
An early age, all folded into a
Receipt (or a lost pawn slip) for a place
That tasted of a human sweetness, laced
With grandeur and improbability —
I passed the old cast-iron hotel where I
Had sat and talked and sipped a cheap cognac
In many a dream, and came out on the fore-
Side of a wide white river promenade
Crossed by a dun-green "L" stark overhead
And paralleled, across the river, by
Another larger elevated steel
Conception of sequoia girders — a
Throg's Neck usurping all the western air
And staining it its brighter green. The east
Bank, though, was still its unprogressed,
Arrested older self. To learn the time,
I detoured down an alleyway between
Two ranks of small, chapfallen shops, and off
A rusty paper rack chained to the steps
Of a moribund grocerette I bought — five cents —
A copy of the Boston *Morning Globe*
For April 7th, 1953.
Northbound again upon the promenade,
I caught an air of spring, a clef or key
Of untuned song, a snatch of melody
In untrained voices carrying no tune
But the light burden of the first warm day
Set loose, light-headed, in the open, to
Salute the single minute of the year
When all's forgiven life, the garroter
Who still stands sentry on the darkening stair
In every stifling rooming house. Alone,
But only literally, I proceed

Past faces that have all the love they need
For once, and can, for once, give some away,
As their smiles give away, their eyes betray,
Level, for once, with mine, and not cast down.
A great glass café, half a riverboat,
Half Crystal Palace, beckons; I step in
To ranks of white enamel tables, wire,
Wood-seated ice-cream-parlor chairs,
And, in the place of honor by the door,
A towering cardboard mockup, like a cake
Of a French battleship, the *Richelieu,*
Around which sailors cluster, jabbering
In French, which figures, since the French fleet's in.
Uproom, in the glass-ceilinged, vasty hall,
Quite like a Continental station, all
The places have been set at an oblong
Long banquet table. As I approach it, all
My dearest friends, looking, in 1953,
Precisely as, in fact, they look today,
Rise from some ambush and, laughing, welcome me
To the fraternal order of the spring.
A pause; an unheard drum roll; from the other side
Of the table steps forth, smiling, Anne, my wife,
And I awaken at twelve-fifty-five
A.M., according to the bedside clock,
On February 14th of this year,
Elated, desolate it could not spell
Me any longer, being but a dream,
Its only evidence being my tears
Of joy or of the other, I can't tell.

Three American Dreams:
A Suite in Phillips House

I. OLD COPY CHIEFS

When Phillips lay in Phillips House, his brain
Drowned in a jigger of his incontinent
Blood, and death's door ajar in front of him,
He dreamt indomitable dreams of death,
Of failure in men's eyes and in his own,
Shut, swollen, on the pillow where pale tubes
Poured air and glucose ever into him.
The first dream saw him out of Phillips House
And back at work in the bone light of his
Old agency, where everything had changed:
Gone his employees, booted, bearded, jeaned
Young copywriters; in their offices,
New reft of Peter Maxes, sat and tapped
On pipes and typewriters a podgy race
Of pawky, dottled former copy chiefs
In faded red suspenders and age-green,
Age-frayed grey-flannel bags, all glad to make
Eight thousand now and be again employed
After so many a winter in a room
Of that sort where one's world's goods creak and shrink
To piles of mildew and one's hair goes grey.
In his own office, Phillips found a man
Like these, but more so, who directed him
To talk to the director, in whose suite
He got his walking papers for the street
Of dreams, where every manliness has its
Distress price, honor is hurt merchandise,
And talents are knocked down and given away.

In life, not far behind his dreams, he was
Discharged one day as cured, the misled blood
Sponged from his brain, and found himself again

Behind his brown desk at the agency,
Still feeble, muscles toneless, memory
Flown over the cuckoo's nest. One afternoon,
Having been summoned to the director's room
Summarily, he was told his work was not
Up to his former standard, and was fired.

II. KID WOMBAT

There is a low-down bar in Phillips House—
Brown-varnished plywood, plastic brewers' signs,
A feral stench of filthy urinals,
Smoke stratified before the blinking blue
Eye of the television jammed by noise
From the contending jukebox—where, between
Sleeping and sleeping, Phillips would repair
To the old world for a greasy glass of beer.
One night in there—or was it day? It's al-
Ways night in there—he was accosted by
A senile, drooling bruiser whose sateen
Battledress jacket read "Kid Wombat" in
Green letters on the back. This dying man—
Râles punctuating his Australian
Subaccent with a rattling, phthisic wheeze—
Did not like Phillips' looks and told him so
And challenged him to a fistfight and lunged
To overtop him and then knocked him down
With a clanging great right cross, and the bar laughed
As one demented throat to see such sport:
The clean young athlete, hated college man,
Supine upon the floor; the leering, brown,
Web-faced old stager gloating over him.

Later, on business in Albany,
Phillips, still fragile as a pullet's egg,
Stopped by a workmen's bar for a quick drink,
And was accosted by a drunk old man

Who challenged him to fight and was talked out
Of it, but only barely, by his friends,
Who sent Phillips packing out into the night
On a hostile street he'd never dreamt of, where
The mystery of life—aloneness—was
Disclosed in full to him and his footfalls.

III. DEATH BY BLACKNESS

In Phillips House old dreams recur. A dream
That visited him first—like an old aunt
In sinister bombazine—at seventeen
Came back to call again. Imagine that
Ink night in Tennessee, when Bessie Smith—
Her forearm crushed on the coaming of her car
When it was sideswiped, then torn off and flung
Into the road behind her—bled to death,
Her voice going out like a guttering candle stump
That breathes its last surrounded by the dark,
Which can afford to wait; imagine that
Old Arthur Rothstein photo of a Ford
Crushed in on some grey, straight Midwestern road,
Its injured driver being comforted
By citizens in a fedora and
A derby hat against the coming night;
Imagine that bright day that Phillips dreamt—
At first at seventeen and once again
In Phillips House—when a vast impact smashed
His father's car, and Phillips, thrown into
A roadside ditch among the thistles, tried
To raise his head, but was prevented by
An access of matt black that overspread
The earth from the horizon, pushing down,
With atmospheres of pressure, his light head
And all the reeds around, a blackness that
Shut, in an undertaker's gesture, his
Blue eyes with black lids, leaving him for dead.

That dream has not come true yet. Knowing what
Inexhaustible patience genuine darkness is
Capable of, I'd say, though, that it will.

II.

Negatives

Hello, black skull. How privily you shine
In all my negatives, white pupils mine
Stock-staring forward under the white shock
Of straw, the surrogate for a forelock
To tug and be made free of Schattenland,
Where dusty Freiherren and Freifrauen stand
About apart in independent pools
Of absolute aphosis by the rules
That govern all reversals. Au contraire,
My awesome, glossy X-rays lay me bare
In whited spades: my skull glows like a moon
Hewn, like a button, out of vivid bone;
The tubular members of my rib cage gleam
Like tortile billets of aluminum;
My hand shines, frozen, like a white batwing
Caught in a strobe. The ordinary thing —
The photo-studio-cabinet-portrait shot,
The positive, quite empty of the not-
So-prepossessing characteristics of
Its subject, featly lighted from above
To maximize the massif of the brow
And minimize the blunt thrust of the prow
Above the smiling teeth clamped on a pipe
In smoking, stiff, still smugness, overripe

To fall — is the extraordinary thing.
When I am dead, my coroners will bring
Not my true bills, those rigorous negatives,
Nor those transparently pure fluorographs,
But this dishonest botch in evidence.
Ecco! they'll say, keeping the wolf far hence.

December 27, 1966

Night sweat: my temperature spikes to 102
At 5 A.M. — a classic symptom — and,
Awake and shaken by an ague, I
Peep out a western window at the worn
Half-dollar of the moon, couched in the rose
And purple medium of air above
The little, distant mountains, a black line
Of gentle ox humps, flanked by greeny lights
Where a still empty highway goes. In Christmas week,
The stars flash ornamentally with the
Pure come-on of a possibility
Of peace beyond all reason, of the spheres
Engaged in an adagio saraband
Of perfect mathematic to set an
Example for the earthly, who abide
In vales of breakdown out of warranty,
The unrepairable complaint that rattles us
To death. Tonight, though, it is almost worth the price —
High stakes, and the veiled dealer vends bad cards —
To see the moon so silver going west,
So ladily serene because so dead,
So closely tailed by her consort of stars,
So far above the feverish, shivering
Nightwatchman pressed against the falling glass.

Homage to Clotho: A Hospital Suite

1

Nowhere is all around us, pressureless,
A vacuum waiting for a rupture in
The tegument, a puncture in the skin,
To pass inside without a password and
Implode us into Erewhon. This room
Is dangerously unguarded: in one wall
An empty elevator clangs its doors,
Imperiously, for fodder; in the hall,
Bare stretchers gape for commerce; in the air
Outside, a trembling, empty brightness falls
In hunger on those whom it would devour
Like any sparrow hawk as darkness falls
And rises silently up the steel stairs
To the eleventh and last floor, where I
Reside on sufferance of authorities
Until my visas wither, and I die.

2

Where is my friend, Rodonda Morton Schiff,
Whose hulk breasts, cygnet-like, the Totensee,
Shrilling her bosun's whistles, piping Death—
The Almirante of the Doldrums in
His black cocked hat and braided cape—aboard
Her scuttling vessel with such poems as just
Escape confounding his gaunt rape with lust?
She should be singing my song at this hour.

3

It is a simple matter to be brave
In facing a black screen with a white FIN —
The final title—fading out as all

Credits have faded in the final crawl,
To which the audience has turned its back
And mumbled, shuffled, struggled into coats
On its way out to face a different night;
It is far harder, in the light of day,
Surrounded by striped student nurses, to
Endure a slight procedure in which you
Are the anatomy lesson in pink paint
Splashed by some master on the tinctured air,
Complete, in gross detail, to the grimace
Denoted by a squiggle on your face
As the bone-marrow needle sinks its fang
Through atomies of drugged and dullard skin
And subcutaneum to pierce the thin,
Tough eggshell of the pelvic arch, wherein —
After steam-hammer pressure — it will suck
Up sips of specimen tissue with a pain
Akin to an extraction under gas,
All gravity against all hollowness.
Affronted and affrighted, I can't pass
This episode in silent dignity
Or bloodless banter; I must sweat and grunt
And moan in corporal fear of corporal pain
Too venial to be mortal, making a fool
Of my lay figure in its textbook pose
(Fig. 1) before these starched and giggling girls
Too young to be let out of simpering school
To meet live terror face to face and lose.

4

Why must the young male nurse who preps the plain
Of my knife-thrower's-target abdomen
With his conversant razor, talking snicks
Of scything into my sedated ears,
Talk also in his flat and friendly voice,
So far from showdowns, on a blasé note

Of reassurance, learnt by classroom rote?
It is that he must make his living, too.

5

If Hell abides on earth this must be it:
This too-bright-lit-at-all-hours-of-the-day-
And-night recovery room, where nurses flit
In stroboscopic steps between the beds
All cheek by jowl that hold recoverers
Suspended in the grog of half-damped pain
And tubularities of light-blue light.
For condiment in this mulled mix, there are
Assorted groans and screams; and, lest repose
Outstrip the sufferer, there is his own
Throat-filling Gobi, mucous membrane gone
Dry as Arabia, as barren of
Hydropsy as a sunburnt cage of bone
Perched on parched rocks where game Parcheesian
(A devil figure, this) went, wended his
Bent way to harvest, for a shekel, rugs,
And pack them back by camel over sands
Of nightmare to transship to richer lands
Where millions of small rills plash into streams
That give rise to great rivers — such wet dreams
Afflict the desiccate on their interminable way
Up through the layers of half-light to day.

6

The riddle of the Sphinx. Man walks on three
Legs at the last. I walk on three, one of
Which is a wheeled I.V. pole, when I rise
From bed the first time to make my aged way
Into the toilet, where, while my legs sway
And the pole sways, swinging its censer high,
I wait to urinate, and cannot make

My mortal coils distill a drop, as time
Stumps past and leaves me swaying there. Defeat:
I roll and hobble back to bed, to the
Refrain of cheeping wheels. Soon the young man
With his snake-handler's fist of catheters
Will come to see me and supply the lack
Of my drugged muscles with the gravity
Of his solution, and I'll void into
A beige bag clipped to the bedside, one of
The bottles, bags, and tubes I'm tethered to
As a condition of continuance.
The body swells until it duns the mind
With importunities in this refined,
White-sheeted torture, practiced by a kind,
Withdrawn white face trained in the arts of love.

7

Home, and the lees of autumn scuttle up
To my halt feet: fat, sportive maple leaves
Struck into ochre by the frost and stripped
From their umbilic cords to skate across
The blacktop drive and fetch up on my shoes
As if including me in their great fall,
Windy with rumors of the coming ice.
Though fallen, frostbit, yellowed also, I
Cannot participate in their late game
But must leave them to hide and seek a place
To decompose in, while I clamber up
Long enneads of stairs to the room where
I'll recompose myself to durance in
A world of voices and surprises, for
As long as Clotho draws my filament—
To my now flagging wonder and applause—
From indefatigable spinnerets,
Until her sister widows, having set
The norms for length and texture of each strand

And sharpened their gross shears, come cut it off
And send me to befriend the winter leaves.

Cancer: A Dream

1. INT.

After the morning shooting, I repair
To my makeshamble dressing room between
The stage and the backstage and the machine
For life support just outside, called a street
And also a location. Inside, air
Is fumed and darkened from a sightless age
Of cave-fish audiences goggling at
Alarms from the direction of the stage,
Now tarnished and festooned with cables. Rage,
Now torn to dated tatters, is replaced
By decorous muttering of a host of crews.
My blacked-out dressing room: a Bernhardt bed,
Swaddled in grubby cloth of gold, holds a
Late *levée* for a rabble of old props —
Drapes, swags, flats, hassocks, bunting, a malign
And lame old vanity with one short leg,
An easel with a bogus portrait of
Some doe-faced buck or beau, a cellarette
Dwarfed by a tottering stack of film cans —
Reclaimed to servitude as furniture.
I feel ungodly weak and sick for noon;
I undress shakily and lie me down
In dust on the vast desert of the bed.

2. INT.

Sound is a kind of pain to which all pain
Responds, as when the prompt boy knocks and calls,

And my insides reply in pain, and I
Sit up in my pyjamas and then stand
And make my way toward the toilet, and,
Returning through a ruinous anteroom
With sand upon the floor and masons' tools,
A length of cast-iron pipe, a dwarf sawhorse,
Discover on the floor, all befouled,
My blue-and-white pyjamas, the immemorial
Stench the pilots smelt in closed cockpits
Over the killing ground above Berlin.
I wash and dress. I walk like a whole man—
The captain on the bridge—to the next scene.

3. EXT.

A visiting fireman. The woman is introduced
By the second-unit man. I miss her name.
She looks familiar. Smokes her cigarette
In a long holder. Waves her hands a lot.
Talks in an accent. Russian. Sixty. Tall.
Not fat but solid. Some kind of beauty once.
Long catlike jawline under jowls. Stiff white
Straight hair tinted a shocking green. Green eyes,
And those not older than before. Nice legs.
Her character comes back. The wife of an
American avant-garde little-magazine
Editor, once a big bug, now passé.
Herself not quite passé—the author of
One book of verse that, less than moribund,
Keeps a fierce toehold on its shelf. Her name
Is Olga Verushkova, and she's here
(Returning to the moment) to research
A piece on movies. Walls of urban air
Weave a small room, made out of light and noise,
Around us and our small talk, which grows dark
And meaning. And, if I were still a man
Of any age, I'd know precisely what

To do when she quite lightly kisses me
Upon the lips and I respond by rote,
And she responds, and I, as if I had
A backbone for my keelson, and were not
Just a façade, a shield upon a stick,
Feel her electric zone impinge on mine
And hear her say, "I am obsessed with you,"
To her amazement, as I break the field
Of force forever, and turn soft away,
One stiffening hand left on her shoulder, and,
Shaking my head to throw the tears away,
Excuse the lateness of the shining hour.

4. EXT.

Dissolve. A rank of crew approaches me.
One tall girl, quite superb in her neat skirt
And modest sweater, looks up from her clip-
Board with grey eyes that will not ever age
And smiles professionally straight at me.
"You're wanted on Stage R. We're running late."
I turn to face the music. I awake.

5. INT.

And go now to the center of the stage
To execute a solo *pas de deux*—
The crab dance—on the black-and-white parquet
Under all eyes and lenses. Partner mine,
With your pink carapace coterminous
With mine, your hard two-fingered hands contained
In mine, your long legs telescoped inside
My legs, your entire *Geist* the work of my
Own brain, why do you lead me such a dance,
So painfully and clumsily drawn out
Of step with the macabre music of
The tiny chamber orchestra that winds,

Diminuendo, down to the last scratch
Of gut, like an old gramophone, leaving
The *premier* — and the only — *danseur* there,
Alone, supine upon the checkered floor,
Where lights — undamped, undimmed — burn on and on,
And eyes — undamped, undimmed — and lenses turn
To other scenes, fresh fields and pastures new,
As I sink into union with you?

Tras Os Montes

I. MOTHER (1892–1973)

My mother, with a skin of crêpe de Chine,
Predominantly yellow-colored, sheer
Enough to let the venous blue show through
The secondarily bluish carapace,
Coughs, rasps, and rattles in her terminal
Dream, interrupted by lucidities,
When, suctioned out and listening with hard
Ears almost waned to stone, she hears me say,
"Mother, we're here. The two of us are here.
Anne's here with me," and she says, "Anne is so —
So pretty," as if abdicating all
Her principalities of prettiness —
So noted in her teens, when she smote all
Who saw her shake a leg upon the stage
Of vaudeville — and sinking into deeps
Where ancience lurks, and barebone toothlessness,
And bareback exits from the centre ring
Of cynosure. Of little, less is left
When we leave: a stick figure of a once
Quite formidable personage. It is,
Therefore, no shock, when next day the call comes
From my worn father, followed by the spade

Engaged upon hard January earth
In Bellevue Cemetery, where he sways
And cries for fifty years of joint returns
Unjointed, and plucks one carnation from
The grave bouquet of springing flowers upon
The medium-priced coffin of veneer,
To press and keep as a venereal
Greenness brought forward from the greying past.

II. FATHER (1895–1974)

Whether the rivals for a wife and mother can
Compose their differences and timely warp
Into concomitant currents, taken by
The selfsame tide when taken at the flood —
Great waters poured black downhill at the height
Of melting in the middle of the night —
Is to be seen. We did not find it so.
My father, whom I loved as if he'd done
All his devoirs (though he had not), and shone
Upon my forehead like a morning sun,
Came home out of his hospital to stay
In our rich, alien house, where trappings tried
His niggard monkishness. Four days he stayed
In his ashen cocoon; the fifth he died
Under my ministrations, his pug jaw
Thrust out toward the port of hopelessness,
Where he (I hope) received the sirens of
All possible welcoming tugs, even as I
Felt under his grey, waxen nose for breath
And called the doctor to record a death
That made shift rather easier for me,
Staring at nothing standing out to sea.

III. Tras Os Montes (197–)

1. In Company

Inspecting their kit and equipment at first light,
I am glad the dawn is behind me, so my friends
Cannot reflect upon my tears. The province I
Move on across the mountains is still night-
Bound, deep beneath the reaches of the sun
Across the passes; so it will remain
All of this long and dusty day, while we—
Will, Joe, Bob, Jonathan, Garth, Peter, Paul,
Ed, John, Phil, Harry, and a droptic me—
March up the sunstruck slopes, dots on the rock
That jags two thousand metres high ahead
Of us above the passes where the dead
Take formal leave of life: a kiss on both
Cheeks of the dear departing, medals stripped,
With all due ceremony, from his breast,
Both epaulets cut loose from their braid stays,
His sword, unbroken, pommelled in the hand
Of his reliever; lastly, a salute
Fired by the arms of officers, the guns
Of other ranks, and a flat bugle call
Played on a battered Spanish instrument
With ragged tassels as the body falls
Over the parapet—gaining weightlessness
As its flesh deliquesces, as its bones
Shiver to ashes—into an air that crawls
With all the arts of darkness far below.

2. A Deux

A new scenario: on upswept slopes
Of ripe green wheat—rare in this country—we
Take, linked, a last long walk. In late July,
The landscape waits, breath bated, on the whim

Of cumulonimbi in the west, which roll
In with deceptive stealth, revealing a
Black heart cut with a cicatrice of fire,
Zigzagging to its ground: a naked peak
Kilometres away, a *serra* out
Of mind. I fix your face with a wax smile.
Our hands articulate our oneness, soon
To dissipate, in a stiff splay of joints.
Is all the language at my tongue's command
Too little to announce my stammered thanks
For your unquestioning hand at my side,
Too much to say I know the lowly deuce
Is a poor card to play beside the ace,
Black with his curlicues and his strong pulse
Of *sauve qui peut* ambition? Calling a spade
A spade, I'm pierced with the extreme regret
Of one who dies intestate; as I'm snatched
Into the stormcloud from the springing field,
From green to black, I spy on you, below,
A lone maid in green wheat, and rain farewells
And late apologies on your grey head,
And thunder sorrows and regrets. The storm
Goes east, and the sun picks out my remains
Against the cloud: a tentative rainbow,
An inverse, weak, and spectral kind of smile.

3. *Alone*

The long march up the fulvous ridgebacks to
The marches, the frontiers of difference —
Where flesh marches with bone, day marches with
His wife the night, and country marches with
Another country — is accomplished best,
By paradox, alone. A world of twos,
Of yangs and yins, of lives and objects, of
Sound grasses and deaf stones, is best essayed
By sole infiltrators who have cast off

Their ties to living moorings, and stand out
Into the roads of noon approaching night
Casting a single shadow, earnest of
Their honorable intention to lay down
Their lives for their old country, humankind,
In the same selfish spirit that inspired
Their lifelong journey, largely and at last
Alone, across the passes that divide
A life from every other, the sheer crags
Of overweening will, the deepening scarps
Like brain fissures that cunningly cut off
Each outcrop from the main and make it one
While its luck lasts, while its bravura holds
Against all odds, until the final climb
Across the mountains to the farther shore
Of sundown on the watersheds, where self,
Propelled by its last rays, sways in the sway
Of the last grasses and falls headlong in
The darkness of the dust it is part of
Upon the passes where we are no more:
Where the recirculating shaft goes home
Into the breast that armed it for the air,
And, as we must expect, the art that there
Turned our lone hand into imperial Rome
Reverts to earth and its inveterate love
For the inanimate and its return.

FINIS

A Note on the Text

For this selection from the published poetry of L. E. Sissman I have relied on the text in *Hello, Darkness: The Collected Poems of L. E. Sissman* (Atlantic–Little, Brown, 1978; Secker and Warburg, 1978). In choosing the contents of this shorter, wieldy book, I found that Sissman's most luminous poetry fell to him in the early and in the very last years of his intensely productive decade, 1964–1974, and was published mainly in the volumes *Dying: An Introduction* (1968) and in the final section of *Hello, Darkness*. *Night Music* contains about half of his published poetry.

A note on L. E. Sissman's other writings: most of the 55 essays Sissman wrote for *The Atlantic Monthly* were published in *Innocent Bystander: The Scene from the 70's* (Vanguard Press, 1975). The literary essays and book reviews he wrote for *The New Yorker* have not yet been collected in book form.

For further writings about Sissman and his work, the curious may seek out my own introduction to *Hello, Darkness* (also reprinted in my book *One of the Dangerous Trades: Essays on the Work and Workings of Poetry*, University of Michigan Press, 1991) and a biographical chapter devoted to Sissman in my book *The Fading Smile: Poets in Boston from Robert Frost to Robert Lowell to Sylvia Plath, 1955–1960* (Knopf, 1994; Norton, 1996). They should also read John Updike's admirable introduction to *Innocent Bystander* and his review of *Hello, Darkness* (*New York Times Book Review*, May 14, 1978); both pieces are included in Updike's *Hugging the Shore*. Other appreciative and insightful essays on Sissman's work include those by Hilton Kramer (*New York Times Book Review*, July 3, 1977), William Pritchard (*Times Literary Supplement*, July 28, 1978), X. J. Kennedy (*Parnassus*, Fall/Winter 1979), Brad Leithauser (*The New Criterion*, October 1983), and Anthony Hecht (*Woodrow Wilson Quarterly*, Winter 1995). Reviews include those by Alfred

Corn (*Yale Review,* Spring 1979), Julian Moynahan (*Washington Post Book World,* June 25, 1978), and Alan Williamson (*Poetry,* November 1978).

Just as L. E. Sissman requested burial in the village of Harvard, Massachusetts, so he left his literary property to Harvard University, pursuant to the death of his wife, Anne, in 1995. His papers and manuscripts are deposited in Harvard's Houghton Library.

PETER DAVISON
October 1998